Hillary Clinton

Other books in the People in the News series:

Beyoncé
Jamie Foxx
Tony Hawk
LeBron James
Angelina Jolie
Ashton Kutcher
Avril Lavigne
Tobey Maguire
Barack Obama
Queen Latifah
J.K. Rowling
Shakira
Tupac Shakur
Ben Stiller
Hilary Swank
Usher

Hillary Clinton

by Dwayne Epstein

LUCENT BOOKS
A part of Gale, Cengage Learning

GALE
CENGAGE Learning

Detroit • New York • San Francisco • New Haven, Conn • Waterville, Maine • London

GALE
CENGAGE Learning·

© 2008 Gale, a part of Cengage Learning

For more information, contact:
Lucent Books
27500 Drake Rd.
Farmington Hills, MI 48331-3535
Or you can visit our Internet site at gale.cengage.com

LIBRARY OF CONGRESS CATALOGING-IN-PUBLICATION DATA

Epstein, Dwayne, 1960–
    Hillary Clinton / by Dwayne Epstein.
        p. cm. — (People in the news)
    Includes bibliographical references and index.
    Audience: Grades 7–10.
    ISBN 978-1-4205-0031-8 (hardcover)
    1. Clinton, Hillary Rodham—Juvenile literature. 2. Presidents' spouses—United States—Biography—Juvenile literature. 3. Legislators—United States—Biography—Juvenile literature. 4. United States. Congress. Senate—Biography—Juvenile literature. 5. Presidential candidates—United States—Biography—Juvenile literature. I. Title.
    E887.C55E67 2008
    328.73092—dc22
    [B]
                                                    2007035910

ISBN-10: 1-4205-0031-7

Printed in the United States of America
2 3 4 5 6 7 12 11 10 09 08

Contents

Foreword   6

Introduction   8
Making the Impossible Possible

Chapter 1   12
In Her Time

Chapter 2   26
"Billary"

Chapter 3   39
From State House to White House

Chapter 4   50
Hillaryland

Chapter 5   66
Casting Her Own Shadow

Chapter 6   77
Race For The White House

Notes   89

Important Dates   95

For More Information   99

Index   104

Picture Credits   111

About the Author   112

Fame and celebrity are fascinating. We are drawn toward people who walk in fame's spotlight, whether they are known for great achievements or for famous acts. The lives of celebrities attract attention, perhaps because their experiences seem in some ways so different from, yet in other ways so similar to, our own.

Newspapers, magazines, and television regularly take advantage of our fascination by running profiles of famous people. For example, television programs such as *Entertainment Tonight* devote all their programming to stories about entertainment and entertainers. Magazines such as *People* fill their pages with stories of the private lives of famous people. Even newspapers, newsmagazines, and television news frequently look at the lives of well-known personalities. But despite the number of articles and programs on offer, few provide us with more than a superficial glimpse of celebrity life.

Lucent's People in the News series offers young readers a closer look at the lives of today's newsmakers, the influences that have shaped them, and the impact they have had on the world, and on other people's lives. The subjects of the series come from many disciplines and walks of life. They include authors, musicians, athletes, political leaders, entertainers, entrepreneurs, and others who have made a mark on modern life and who, in many cases, will continue to do so for years to come.

These biographies are more than just factual accounts. Each book emphasizes the contributions, achievements, or deeds that have brought fame to the individual. The books also show how that person has influenced modern life. Authors describe their subjects in a realistic, unsentimental light. For example, Bill Gates—the cofounder and chief executive officer of the software giant Microsoft—has made personal computers the most vital tool of the modern age. Few dispute his business skills, his perseverance, or his technical expertise, but critics say he is ruthless in his dealings with competitors and is driven more by his desire to maintain Microsoft's dominance in the computer industry than by an interest in furthering technology.

In these books, young readers will encounter inspiring stories about real people who have achieved success despite enormous obstacles. Oprah Winfrey—the most powerful, most watched, and wealthiest woman on television today—spent the first six years of her life in the care of her grandparents while her unwed mother sought work and a better life elsewhere. Her adolescence was colored by promiscuity, pregnancy at age fourteen, rape, and sexual abuse.

Each author documents and supports his or her work with a selection of primary and secondary source quotations taken from diaries, letters, speeches, and interviews. All quotes are footnoted to show readers exactly how and where biographers got their information, and provide guidance for further research. The quotations bring the text to life by giving readers eyewitness accounts of the life and achievements of each person covered in the People in the News series.

In addition, each book in the series includes photographs, annotated bibliographies, timelines, and comprehensive indexes. For both the casual reader and the student researcher, the People in the News series offers an insight into the lives of today's newsmakers—people who shape the way we live, work, and play in the modern age.

Making the Impossible Possible

When Hillary Rodham Clinton graduated from Wellesley College in 1969 she was the first student in the school's long and illustrious history to give a commencement address. It proved to be one of many groundbreaking firsts for the young woman now considered the most famous woman in the world. In part of her speech, she defined what she saw as her generation's greatest challenge: "The challenge now is to practice politics as the art of making what appears to be impossible, possible."[1] For the remainder of her life she herself would strive to do exactly that.

Opportunist Or Advocate?

Hillary Rodham Clinton has broken down an amazing amount of barriers long thought to be impossible to breach. She became the first female lawyer in her firm; the first working First Lady in the state of Arkansas; the only First Lady ever elected to public office; the first female senator from the state of New York; and the first woman to mount a serious campaign to become President of the United States.

None of these impressive accomplishments were achieved easily. Clinton was forced to confront sexism, discrimination, and unfair treatment every step of the way. The result of dealing

Hillary Clinton has become one of the most famous women in American history by breaking down barriers in her long, illustrious career.

Clinton has been an advocate for children's rights in many different countries around the world.

with such confrontations has created many political enemies who consider her to be, among other things, opportunistic: Someone who seeks to take advantage of a situation for their own personal gain.

This might even be true if it were not for the fact that the issue she has fought for all of her life has remained consistent from the beginning. In her bestselling book *It Takes A Village*, she stated it plainly:

> I'm often asked what I would like to see happen above all else in our country and in our world. There are so many things to pray for.... But certainly my answer would be a world in which all children are loved and cared for—first by the families into which they are born, and then by all of us who are linked to them and to one another.[2]

As an advocate, or one who supports the cause, for children and families for more than forty years, she has achieved a great amount. She has accomplished this in many ways, first as an idealistic law student, and then a lawyer, a mother, a teacher, a politician, even as an author of several bestselling books. Hardly perfect, she herself readily admits to making high profile mistakes, such as her contentious relationship with the media and her inability to work with political opponents, causing the failure of national health care reform in 1994. She was also the only First Lady forced to testify before a grand jury amid the scandals of her husband's administration.

She has since dealt with much of the stereotyping that was leveled against her and learned some important lessons along the way. As early as 1992 she attempted to demonstrate those lessons when her opponents were calling her names and attacking her character. At the time she said, "Let's reach across the lines that divide us not with pointing fingers but outstretched hands."[3]

The Last Great Hurdle

She has of course not always achieved the goal of maintaining an outstretched hand. However, with time she learned to look beyond the petty bickering of politics and see clearly the goal she intends to achieve. She is more aware of the pitfalls of public service and what it take survive.

As a recently elected senator, she was asked what advice she could give young women considering a life in politics. She said, "My message to young women is that, as tough as the political environment is, if you care about making a difference, you have to be willing to get out there and try. .... We've broken through all of these barriers so that individual women can make the choice that's right for them."[4]

With goals clearly sought and equipped with the tools to achieve them, Hillary Clinton is now prepared to confront the greatest impossibility of them all; the idea that any little girl in America can grow up to be President of the United States.

In Her Time

When discussing important individuals, historians often debate whether the times made the individual or the individual made the times. In the case of Hillary Clinton it is a combination of both the individual and the time coming together in perfect unison. There is also much that transpired before she was born that helped create the era in which she lived and influenced. As a typical yet distinct product of the postwar generation, Hillary Rodham Clinton developed into a politically and socially active woman due to a combination of the influential groundwork laid by the women who came before her, her own life experiences, and most importantly, her own natural ability.

Dorothy and Hugh

Her mother Dorothy Emma Howell Rodham proved to be one of the most important influences in her life. Born into a time when women were considered second-class citizens, she survived an abusive childhood with a firm belief in social justice and an open heart to those less fortunate. Dorothy Howell was born in 1919 in Chicago to parents who often left her to fend for herself. Her parents divorced in 1927 and her mother sent Dorothy and her younger sister to live with their grandmother in California.

By the time she was fourteen she was working for a family with two young children in exchange for living quarters and three dollars a week. When Dorothy graduated high school her plans for college were abandoned when her mother asked her to return to Chicago to work as her housekeeper. Years later Hillary asked her

Dorothy Rodham, Hillary's mother, was one of the most significant influences in her life.

mother why she returned and Dorothy told her: "I'd hoped so hard that my mother would love me that I had to take the chance and find out. When she didn't, I had nowhere else to go."[5]

Hillary's father, Hugh Rodham, survived the tough industrial environs of Scranton, Pennsylvania due to his iron-willed mother, Hannah. A childhood accident nearly resulted in the amputation of both of his legs but his mother stood firm against the medical establishment and nursed him back to health herself.

Hugh Rodham inherited his mother's iron determination, graduating from Penn State during the height of the Depression with a degree in physical education. He then went to Chicago without telling his parents and found a job selling drapery fabrics around the Midwest. It was on the job as a traveling

Political Terminology

Growing up in a home with politically aware parents, Hillary early on knew the use and practice of these terms:

Progressive/Traditionalist: *Progressive* refers to an individual or a movement that favors progress over tradition, often arrived at through successive steps. A traditionalist wishes to maintain the existing way of things.

Conservatism: A general preference for the existing order of society and in opposition to efforts to bring about sharp change.

Liberalism: A viewpoint or an ideology (a set of ideas) associated with free political institutions as well as support for a strong role of government in regulations.

Left Wing/Right Wing: Terms for political ideologies that originated in England, based on the seating in Parliament, which featured seats on two sides of an aisle. The left wing holds the view that there are unacceptable social inequalities in the present order of society. The right wing supports the current order of things or a return to an earlier order of things.

Republican/Democrat: The two main political parties in America. Both have various viewpoints, but it is largely held that the majority of Republicans are conservative while the majority of Democrats are more liberal. The Republican Party is older and is often referred to as the Grand Old Party, or GOP.

Partisan/Bipartisan: Usually in reference to Congress, *partisan* refers to one specific party banding together on an issue, while *bipartisan* refers to both parties coming together in unity.

E.D. Hirsch Jr., Joseph F. Kett, James Trefil, *The Dictionary of Cultural Literacy*, 2nd edition. New York: Houghton Mifflin, 1993.

salesman that he met a pretty young woman applying for a job as a clerk typist. Following a lengthy courtship, Dorothy Howell and Hugh Rodham married in 1942 shortly after the bombing of Pearl Harbor. With America's entry into World

War II, Hugh Rodham enlisted in the navy, became a chief petty officer stationed near Lake Michigan and trained young men in self-defense. When he could, he would visit Dorothy in their small Chicago apartment.

When the war ended in 1945, Hugh started his own drapery business and, along with Dorothy, began doing what most reunited couples in America were doing: raising a family. Adding to the baby boom the country was experiencing was Dorothy and Hugh Rodham's first child, Hillary Diane Rodham born October 26, 1947 in Chicago's Edgewater Hospital. Younger brother Tony followed in 1950 and 1954 saw the arrival of another brother named Hugh. Economically it was the postwar boom and Hugh Rodham's small yet successful drapery business that allowed him to move his family to the middle-class Illinois suburb of Park Ridge when Hillary was almost three.

Best of Both Worlds

Hillary's parents provided for her and her brothers so that they lived comfortably in their middle class existence. A highlight was the summers spent at their cabin in Pennsylvania near the Pocono Mountains. Emotionally, the Rodhams instilled important values in their children. Dorothy underscored compassion and individuality, especially to her daughter. Years later her mother said, "I was determined that no daughter of mine was going to have to go through the agony of being afraid to say what she had on her mind."[6]

Hillary absorbed the example of her parents' values. They were exhibited through Hugh's tough but fair assessment of the ways of the world and melded with Dorothy's equally heartfelt belief in her daughter's individuality. "I have a family that from the very beginning of my life said to me, 'You are a valuable and special person,'" Hillary would remember. "And they also said to me, 'You may be a girl but you can do whatever you choose to do.'..."[7]

Early on, Hillary exhibited natural leadership ability and resourcefulness as she helped raise her two younger brothers, worked in her father's business, and organized other neighborhood children in fundraising events. This was accomplished while she

Hugh and Dorothy Rodham instilled important values in their children and have supported Hillary's career and political aspirations.

also excelled in school and church activities. According to Dorothy, "She was already a perfectionist when she was eight. She always set very high standards for herself. She was almost scary."[8]

As a little girl Hillary was a self-described tomboy who made friends easily in her suburban neighborhood and took to the role of natural leader quite comfortably. She quickly absorbed the virtues of her mother's kindness and her father's tenacity. She also found herself the recipient of another aspect of her father's personality that exists to this day: "I inherited his laugh, the same big rolling guffaw that can turn heads in a restaurant and send cats running from the room," remembers Hillary.[9]

A Different World

The world Hillary knew as a child was in some ways radically different than the one that exists today. Other than a deep-rooted resentment of Communism in the world, the country was booming throughout the 1950s in both finances and spirit. Television existed but the Rodhams discouraged their children from watching it and instead played imaginative word games created by Dorothy. Hillary and her friends could roam their neighborhood after school without a fear of strangers or criminal activity, save for the occasional bully. Overall, the mood of the country created a sense of endless possibility for any child.

This was not entirely true for many young women who were still taught that their place was strictly in the home. Hillary discovered this when her dreams of being an astronaut were dashed in a response to a letter she sent to the newly formed National Aeronautics and Space Administration. The letter said girls were not accepted into the program, which disheartened Hillary a great

Dealing with a Bully

In this excerpt from Hillary Clinton's autobiography, she relates a story from her early years that demonstrated her courage:

"Shortly after we moved to Park Ridge, my mother noticed that I was reluctant to go outside to play. Sometimes I came in crying, complaining that the girl across the street was always pushing me around. Suzy O'Callaghan had older brothers, and was used to playing rough. I was four years old, but my mother was afraid that if I gave in to my fears, it would set a pattern for the rest of my life. One day, I came running into the house. She stopped me.

'Go back out there,' she ordered, 'and if Suzy hits you, you have my permission to hit her back. You have to stand up for yourself. There's no room in this house for cowards.' She later told me she watched from behind the dining room curtain as I squared my shoulders and marched across the street.

I returned a few minutes later, glowing with victory. 'I can play with the boys,' I said. 'And Suzy will be my friend!'

She was and still is."

Hillary Rodham Clinton, *Living History*. New York: Simon & Schuster, 2003, p. 12.

deal. She was slightly consoled by the fact that her poor eyesight would have disqualified her anyway in spite of her gender.

Her mother still encouraged her dreams and hoped her daughter might some day become the country's first female Supreme Court Justice. Her father made sure she and her brothers worked hard to succeed at whatever they did. According to her brother Tony, "We'd rake the leaves, cut the grass, pull the weeds, shovel snow. After your errands you'd walk in and say, 'Gee dad, I could use two or three dollars.' He'd flop another potato on the plate and say, 'That's your reward.'"[10]

Early Advocate for Children

These life lessons manifested themselves in Hillary's excellent grades in school as well as her other endeavors. She won several merit badges for community service in the Girl Scouts, played piano, took ballet lessons and also played competitive sports. Of all the activities she undertook, the ones closest to her heart involved working with children. Her natural leadership ability, coupled with her father's determination and her mother's compassion, resulted in a lifelong devotion to children:

> From the time I was a child myself, I loved being around children, looking into their faces or listening to the stories they told. Like many firstborn children, I learned to care for children by baby-sitting my two younger brothers. As a teenager, I baby-sat for other children too, and at thirteen I got my first 'real' job, supervising children at a park on summer mornings. Through my church, I helped care for the children of migrant farmworkers while their parents labored in the fruit orchards and vegetable fields near my home ...[11]

The church to which she and her family belonged was another influential aspect of Hillary's formative years. As a regular churchgoer of Park Ridge's First United Methodist Church, she strove to live up to the motto of one of Methodism founders, John Wesley: "Do all the good you can, by all the means you can, in all the ways you can, as long as you can." [12]

Early in her life, Hillary realized that working with children was one of the causes closest to her heart.

The University of Life

Helping Hillary put these words into action was a new youth minister named Don Jones who arrived in 1961 demonstrating faith through social action. As a young teen, she was influenced greatly by Jones, whose example she still follows to this day. His weekend youth meetings were dubbed the University of Life and broke with the church's traditional way of doing things. In order to show his young flock the importance of Wesley's words, he organized excursions into Chicago's many black ghettos where Hillary and her other white middle-class classmates encountered abject poverty for the first time.

Spirituality and the Church have always been important to Hillary, pictured here leaving Palm Sunday Mass with President Clinton, center, and Cardinal Roger Mohony.

Jones would then organize projects so that Hillary and the other pupils could see the effect of charity at work. The children of Hispanic migrant workers in Park Ridge were cared for by the Methodist Church students who helped them learn English. Jones also inspired Hillary with volumes of classic and contemporary books on theology and philosophy. Her most cherished memory remains a field trip Jones organized to hear another young minister named Martin Luther King speak in favor of racial equality. Afterwards, Jones introduced the awestruck Hillary to the charismatic Baptist minister.

Consequently, Hillary always credited Jones for her devotion to the underprivileged but he modestly credits Hillary's innate spirituality. "This may sound corny but the key to understanding Hillary is her spiritual center," said Jones. "Unlike some people who at a particular age land on a cause and become concerned, with Hillary I think of a continuous textual development. Her social concern and her political thought rest on a spiritual foundation."[13]

Differing Politics

Hillary's ongoing development also included politics. Her father's conservative Republican beliefs and her mother's liberal Democratic views exposed her to different political points of view. As her family watched John F. Kennedy's funeral procession on television in shock and horror, Dorothy secretly admitted to Hillary that she had voted for the assassinated young president without Hugh's knowledge.

Throughout her years in high school Hillary kept a high profile as a Republican supporter, even going so far as to work for conservative Barry Goldwater's failed presidential campaign in 1964. She sported campaign regalia as a Goldwater Girl but was forced to see the other point of view when her teacher assigned her the role of Democratic candidate Lyndon Johnson in a class debate. Outwardly, she sided with many of her conservative school teachers and her father, a child of the Depression who believed anyone could make it if they worked hard enough.

Inwardly, she began to have doubts, due in large part to the influence of Rev. Jones, the events of the 60s that continued to unfold, and her mother's belief that Hillary could achieve as well as any boy.

In the midst of all this, she still managed to be a typical teen who swooned and screamed with her friends when The Beatles and The Rolling Stones appeared on television. As First Lady she said, "Years later, when I met icons from my youth, like Paul McCartney, George Harrison [of The Beatles] and Mick Jagger [of The Rolling Stones], I didn't know whether to shake hands or jump up and down squealing."[14]

Welcome to Wellesley

Much that has been written about Hillary Clinton's early years paints a picture of a classic overachiever. This certainly appeared to be the case when she graduated in 1965 from Maine South High School in the top five percent of her class. She had her choice of colleges narrowed down to Smith and Wellesley, two of the so-called Seven Sisters of all-girl schools. Her mother showed no preference but her father insisted that whichever she chose it would not be full of what he considered no-good loafers. For no particular reason Hillary chose Wellesley in Massachusetts.

Her entry into college coincided with an escalation of events that marked the decade as one of the most tumultuous in modern American history. The youth of the country had more material wealth than any generation before them which allowed them to question many long held traditions that they considered to be out of date. As Hillary studied diligently, America's involvement in the Vietnam War divided the nation. Other divisions began to erupt between young and old, rich and poor, black and white, even among men and women.

When she was in high school, Hillary had stated her ambition was to marry a senator. While in college, Hillary started a chapter of the Young Republicans, however she and her classmates shifted their focus to the alarming events around them that continued at a jarring pace. One of the most disturbing to the young

Hillary was an influential student at Wellesley College in Massachusetts and gave a passionate speech at her graduation ceremony.

student was the assassination of Dr. Martin Luther King. The idealistic and charismatic speaker Hillary had met was murdered in Memphis, leaving her and the rest of the nation to question much of their core beliefs.

National Recognition

College campuses were a major center for the exchange of ideas and Hillary's dorm room became a hub of activity among her fellow students. They discussed the daily events affecting the nation and Hillary was often the most articulate among them. Her thesis at Wellesley reflected her evolving ideals as she questioned the use of violent activism during the Vietnam War, which she now openly opposed.

Prior to her graduation on May 31, 1969, Hillary was approached by a group of fellow students about delivering the commencement address. In the long and prestigious history of Wellesley many notable individuals had spoken but no student had ever done so at graduation. School president Ruth Adams opposed the idea on the grounds that it had never been done. Hillary suggested that might be reason enough to at least try. After considerable thought, Hillary was granted the right to speak.

By 1969, several more prominent individuals were assasinated, such as Black Muslim leader Malcolm X and presidential candidate Robert Kennedy, younger brother of the slain president, John F. Kennedy. The Civil Rights, Environmental, and Women's Movements raged on and, most explosive of all, the Vietnam War caused rioting in the streets of America. All of these events and much more were in the mind of Hillary Rodham as she prepared the text of her speech.

Her parents had planned to attend but unfortunately, her mother was not well and was advised not to travel. Hugh Rodham would not go alone and told Hillary he would stay in Illinois and tend to Dorothy. Hillary was disappointed but understood. Dorothy was even more disappointed in not being able to see her only daughter realize the dream of graduating from a major university.

Hillary's speech, like others heard on college campuses that year, was both thought provoking and memorable. In part of her speech she said, "And so our questions, our questions about our institutions, about our colleges, about our churches, about our government, continue."[15]

The result was a seven-minute standing ovation. The text of her speech was even reprinted in Life Magazine. Her father had flown into Boston the night before, stayed near the airport, took the train to the campus the next day to see her speech, congratulated his daughter and her friends, and then traveled right back to Park Ridge. "All that mattered to me was that he made it to my graduation," she said, "which helped diminish the disappointment I felt over my mother's absence. In many ways, this moment was as much hers as mine."[16]

Chapter 2

"Billary"

As a young woman, Hillary Rodham was very aware that the options that lay before her were vastly different than those of her mother's generation. Hillary took advantage of the changing role of women as she moved into the public spotlight through Bill Clinton's political aspirations and her own work advocating for children. The result, in partnership with Bill Clinton, would be a lifelong balancing act between progressive ideas and traditional standards.

Yale Law School

Hillary Rodham had her pick of any Ivy League school after receiving her Bachelor of Arts degree in political science from Wellesley. Her thesis work exploring social activism had her leaning toward a law degree, feeling that she could advocate best for children and families by working as a lawyer. Her application was accepted by both Harvard and Yale the year before she graduated from Wellesley.

Her decision was finalized when a Harvard student introduced her to one of his law professors. The professor was told of Hillary's choice of either Harvard or its major rival. The professor responded that Harvard has no rival, nor does it need any more women. "I was leaning toward Yale anyway but this encounter removed any doubts about my choice," said Hillary.[17]

The young woman with the overly thick glasses and preference for jeans and baggy shirts impressed many with her quick and agile mind on the stately New Haven, Connecticut campus of Yale.

The fact that she had gained national attention with her Wellesley address added to her growing reputation when she started classes in the fall of 1969. She was one of only twenty-seven female students out of a student body of 235. The times were changing and Hillary Rodham was determined to be involved in the change.

Hillary utilized her massive reserves of energy and resourcefulness to excel in both her class work and outside activities. She served on the editorial board of the Yale Review of Law and Social Action and also cultivated an important relationship with Marian Wright Edelman. Edelman was a Yale graduate who became the first black woman to pass the bar exam in the state of Mississippi and worked as a civil rights lawyer when she met Hillary in the spring of 1970. Hillary volunteered to work for Edelman's advocacy group for children, which would eventually become

While at Yale, Hillary Rodham embarked on a long friendship with civil rights lawyer and children's advocate Marian Wright Edelman.

The Children's Defense Fund

Hillary worked for the Children's Defense Fund (CDF), starting in college and until she became U.S. First Lady. The organization is still a viable and important advocate for children. Hillary served as CDF chair from 1986 to 1992. Their web site states the following background information:

"The Children's Defense Fund's mission is to ensure every child a Healthy Start, a Head Start, a Fair Start, a Safe Start, and a Moral Start in life and successful passage to adulthood with the help of caring families and communities.

CDF provides a strong, effective voice for all the children of America who cannot vote or speak for themselves. We pay particular attention to the needs of poor and minority children and those with disabilities. CDF encourages preventive investment before they get sick or into trouble, drop out of school, or suffer family breakdown.

CDF began in 1973 and is a private, nonprofit organization supported by foundation and corporate grants and individual donations. We have never taken government funds.

The Children's Defense Fund grew out of the Civil Rights Movement under the leadership of Marian Wright Edelman. It has become the nation's strongest voice for children and families since its founding in 1973. CDF traces its heritage to Dr. Martin Luther King Jr., his Poor People's Campaign and the Washington Research Project, a nonprofit organization that monitored federal programs for low-income families."

Source: http://www.childrensdefense.org/site/PageServer?pagename=About_ CDF.

The Children's Defense Fund. Hillary received a grant and this, along with her scholarship, is what she lived on at Yale. That summer she gained valuable experience researching the plight of migrant worker's children for a congressional committee headed by Minnesota Senator and future Vice-President Walter Mondale.

The Boy From Hope

When Hillary returned to classes in the fall she was more convinced then ever that her life's work would be to benefit underprivileged and abused children. Her research work and other campus projects continued to impress those around her. One such impressed fellow student was a charismatic Arkansas native and Rhodes scholar with lofty political aspirations named Bill Clinton. Sporting what she called a "Viking beard" while in his first year at Yale, Hillary had noticed Bill Clinton early in the year boasting about the size of watermelons in his hometown of Hope, Arkansas.

While doing research in the library, Hillary had seen the young man staring at her more than a few times. On one such occasion, he was in conversation with another student when Hillary took the initiative and approached Bill, stating, "If you're going to keep staring at me and I'm going to keep staring back, we ought to at least know each other's names. Mine's Hillary Rodham. What's yours?"[18]

The two began a casual conversation that continued on for some time. When Hillary saw Bill again a few days later, the conversation easily picked up where it had left off. According to Clinton:

> I was determined to spend some time with her. She said she was going to register for next term's classes so I said I'd go, too. We stood in line and talked. I thought I was doing pretty well until we got to the front of the line. The registrar looked up at me and said, 'Bill, what are you doing back here? You registered this morning.' I turned beet red and Hillary laughed that big laugh of hers.[19]

After registering, the law students spent the day at a nearby art museum and then discovered even more about each other. Hillary learned of Bill's desire for public service in the political arena and his background growing up in Arkansas. His father had died in a car accident before he was born, forcing his mother Virginia to raise him on her own with the help of her family while she finished nursing school. She later remarried, and Bill and his

After All These Years

Hillary Clinton wrote in her life story what it was about Bill Clinton that attracted her to him at first and remains so to this day:

> "I was starting to realize that this young man from Arkansas was much more complex than first impressions might suggest. To this day, he can astonish me with the connections he weaves between ideas and words and how he makes it all sound like music. I still love the way he thinks and the way he looks. One of the first things I noticed about Bill was the shape of his hands. His wrists are narrow and his fingers tapered and deft, like those of a pianist or surgeon. When we first met as students, I loved watching him turn the pages of a book. Now his hands are showing signs of age after thousands of handshakes and golf swings and miles of signatures. They are, like their owner, weathered but still expressive, attractive and resilient."

Hillary Rodham Clinton, *Living History*. New York: Simon & Schuster, 2003, pp. 53–54.

younger half-brother Roger managed to survive the often abusive behavior of his stepfather. Bill and Hillary began to see each other exclusively by the end of the semester and as both have stated, the conversation they started over thirty years ago continues to this day.

Meet The Parents

As their heavy load of classes continued, Bill and Hillary saw more and more of each other. When the summer break arrived, Bill had convinced Hillary to join him in working for George McGovern's ill-fated Democratic Presidential campaign. Although

Hillary began dating another ambitious law student, Bill Clinton. The two worked together on George McGovern's presidential campaign in 1972.

she left the Republican Party while at Wellesley, Hillary was still politically active and found the Democratic Party more in line with her own beliefs. Clinton managed McGovern's campaign in Texas while Hillary diligently registered Hispanic voters in the state during the 1972 campaign. The two idealistic yet practical law students were clearly falling in love.

When it came time to meet each other's parents it played out like scenes from a TV or movie comedy. Most of Hillary's family took to Bill except for her father, a lifelong Midwestern Republican highly skeptical of the charming young Southern Democrat. Over time, Bill did win him over, even to the point that Hugh Rodham worked on some of Bill's campaigns.

When Hillary went to Arkansas to meet Virginia Clinton the results were even more comical. Mrs. Clinton was a woman who always dressed with a certain flair and had a striking gray streak in her hair. In contrast, Hillary rarely wore dresses and the day before meeting Virginia she had mangled her own hair in a botched attempt to style it. The meeting had both women less than impressed with the other. According to Bill:

> I got a kick out of watching them try to figure each other out. Over time they did, as mother came to care less about Hillary's appearance and Hillary came to care more about it. Underneath their different styles, they were both smart, tough, resilient, passionate women. When they got together, I didn't stand a chance.[20]

After Yale

Although Hillary started at Yale a year before Bill, she graduated the same year as Clinton because she took an extra year to work at Yale's Child Study Center, adding to her studies with child psychology and family law classes. Her work resulted in important research used in a book co-written by Anna Freud, among others, entitled *Beyond the Best Interests of the Child*. She also worked diligently at the Carnegie Council on Children and the Children's Defense Fund with Marian Wright Edelman. Her impressive work earned her a Juris Doctor Degree from Yale in 1973.

Following their graduation, Bill and Hillary made plans to keep in touch but had commitments elsewhere. Bill returned to Arkansas to teach law and Hillary became a staff attorney with the Children's Defense Fund in Cambridge, Massachusetts. They stayed in touch by phone and lengthy visits but the need to be in constant contact was almost overwhelming. Their work was important to each of them but their feelings for each other were equally important.

While they continued to grapple with their feelings, Hillary was offered an important legal position. During the 1972 presidential campaign several burglars were caught breaking into Democratic headquarters in Washington's Watergate Hotel. Although Republican President Richard Nixon easily won reelection, the

During the Watergate scandal that caused President Richard Nixon to resign, Rodham (pictured center) was part of the staff assigned to determine whether there were legal grounds to impeach the president.

ongoing investigation of the Watergate break-in and its subsequent cover-up revealed a trail that eventually led to President Nixon. A Senate judiciary committee was put in charge of pursuing legal grounds for impeachment of the president. One of the three women lawyers out of a staff of forty-three was Hillary Rodham. She was charged with researching facts to determine the president's guilt strictly on a legal basis without personalizing the case in any way. Eventually the staff disbanded when President Nixon became the first president to resign in office on August 8, 1974.

Following Her Heart

Following Nixon's resignation, Hillary's work investigating the impeachment earned her an enhanced reputation in the legal community. She had her choice of joining any prestigious legal firm in the country, which would have earned her hundreds of thousands of dollars a year. Friends, colleagues and family members all encouraged her in that direction but she also received an offer that was even more enticing to her.

Back in Arkansas Bill Clinton contacted Hillary in Washington and asked her to join him on the teaching staff of the University of Arkansas School of Law in Fayetteville. On the surface the offer may not have seemed as enticing as joining a high-level law firm or even returning to the Children's Defense Fund, which Hillary was also considering. Friends and family were advising her not to go but ultimately the decision was Hillary's to make. "I just finally decided, you know, this is no way to make a decision," said Hillary. "When you love somebody, you just have to go and see what it's like."[21]

Her life-altering decision to go to Arkansas was also based on her evolving conflict over being a public advocate for what she

After weighing various career options, Hillary decided to follow her heart and move to Arkansas to help Bill launch his campaign for a seat in Congress.

believed in or working within the political system to enact the policy changes she felt were important. Bill Clinton, who felt much the same way she did about important issues, helped her with her conflict. She arrived in Arkansas on a hot August night in 1974 and within 48 hours she was teaching at the same school as Bill, running a legal aid clinic, and also helping Bill with his newly launched campaign for a seat in Congress.

Her life in Arkansas was vastly different than anything she had experienced before. Growing up in suburban Illinois, living in Eastern colleges, and working for high powered law firms in Washington did not prepare her for small town life in the rural south. When one of her students had not been in class for a few days she dialed information to get his home phone number. The operator knew the student and told Hillary the young man had gone camping. "I had never before lived in a place so small, friendly and Southern and I loved it," she said. She even enjoyed the school's trademark rallying cry: "I went to Arkansas Razorback football games and learned to 'call the hogs.'"[22]

Retail Politics

Hillary's other responsibility also moved her closer toward policy change in the political arena instead of public advocacy. She had worked on campaigns before but Bill Clinton's run for the fourth congressional district gave the race a vested interest because of her personal involvement with the candidate. The district was a long held seat by Republican John Paul Hammerschmidt and even though Clinton lost, he came closer than any other Democrat had before. He lost by a mere four percentage points.

Part of his success was due in large part to Hillary. Bill was a natural when it came to going out and meeting and greeting voters, which is often referred to as retail politics. Hillary's strength was her amazing organizational skills which she used to run Bill's campaign. Together they made an impressive team and proved it by winning when Bill ran for state attorney general in 1976. Bill's rule to his staff was simple and direct: "Anything Hillary says, do it. She's the smartest woman I ever met."[23]

Together Bill and Hillary made an impressive couple and campaign team and they married on October 11, 1975.

Hillary's decisions at this time in her life were not made lightly even though her friends and family shook their heads in disbelief at some of her choices. When she visited friends in Illinois during the summer of 1975 and caught up with their lives, it was confirmed that her choice was the right one. When she returned, Bill met her at the airport and said, "You know that little house you said you liked? Well, I bought it. Now you have to marry me."[24] The house in Fayetteville was to Hillary's liking but the proposal made her pause. Then, on October 11, 1975, in the presence of friends and family, Bill and Hillary were married in the house he bought for her.

Political and Legal Ascent

The following year, Bill's successful run for state attorney general made him the youngest such official in the state. For Hillary, taking on the dual roles of politician's wife and successful career woman was difficult but extremely rewarding. Bill's ascent into Arkansas politics meant a move to Little Rock and greater responsibilities, not the least of which was working on Jimmy Carter's presidential campaign. Bill managed the campaign in Arkansas and Hillary agreed to work in Indiana.

As Indiana's field coordinator, Hillary was required to get out the Democratic votes in the heavily Republican state. This meant getting important data from the men who ran Indiana's Democratic Party, so she set up a meeting to do just that. As the only woman at a table of drunken men, she repeatedly asked them for the information. One of the men grabbed her by the neck, yelled at her to just do her job, and that would be the end of it. With her heart pounding in her chest she removed his hand and told the man, "First, don't ever touch me again. Second, if you were as fast with the answers to my questions as you are with your hands I'd have the information I need to do my job."[25]

Carter did not win Indiana but he did win the election, but by that time Hillary had other commitments. She began working as the first female lawyer at the Rose Law Firm, in Little Rock, Arkansas and was now making more money than her husband. President Carter was aware of her work for his campaign and appointed her to the board of his newly formed Legal Services Corporation. The board would provide financial services to legal aid clinics throughout the country. As if this were not enough work for the productive young lawyer, she also founded and presided over the Arkansas Advocates for Children and Families. This advocacy group was organized not for profit but to provide legal help for low-income families.

Clinton was the first female lawyer at Rose Law Firm in Little Rock, Arkansas and continued to work there through her husband's campaign for governor.

She still managed to work in the dual arenas of public advocacy and political policy. Policy came in the form of her husband's decision to run for governor. If all of this was not enough, Hillary was forced to scale back on her casework for another new responsibility. In February of 1980, Bill and Hillary planned to welcome the birth of their daughter.

Chapter 3

From State House To White House

Hillary Rodham Clinton continued to deal with the delicate balance required to be both a politician's wife and a career woman. Some of her husband's adversaries saw the balance she attempted as a conflict between being a traditional role model and the progressive ideals of being a lawyer. This would play out on a much larger stage when her husband entered the presidential race.

Arkansas's Youngest Governor

Bill Clinton's term as attorney general of Arkansas became a springboard for much greater political aspirations that required a great deal of help from Hillary. In 1978, Bill launched his campaign for state governor and along with his young and eager staff he relied heavily on the advice of his wife.

She helped her husband's campaign while her work with the Rose Law Firm continued. Her successful legal work even afforded them a house in the upper-middle-class suburb of Hillcrest. Her appearance also evolved from her college days since being a lawyer meant forsaking her jeans and baggy shirts. A shorter hairstyle, more professional attire and the chance to wear contact lenses in place of glasses gave her a much more professional demeanor. "I tried wearing contacts from the time I was sixteen-years-old and I never could get them to work," she said. "I have terrible

In 1978, thirty-two-year-old Bill Clinton became the youngest governor in Arkansas history.

eyesight. Those glasses were very, very huge. Then they came out with soft, thinner contacts, and it was like a miracle to me."[26]

This new look, but mostly her impressive organizational skills, went a long way in helping her husband win the election. He defeated his Republican opponent by a margin of almost two to one. The home in Hillcrest was now replaced with a move into the governor's mansion, as thirty-two-year-old Clinton became the youngest governor in Arkansas history.

Hillary broke new ground as well, becoming the first working First Lady in the history of the state. The following year Hillary's career also took an upward turn. She went from being her firm's only female lawyer to the firm's first female full partner, still earning more money than her husband, the governor. The Clintons then decided it was time for a long overdue vacation.

Chelsea Morning

Bill and Hillary took their vacation in Europe, with a lengthy portion of it taking place in England. Bill showed Hillary many of his old hangouts when he was a young student at Oxford. "One day as we window-shopped down King's Road in Chelsea," said Clinton, "The loudspeaker of a store blared out Judy [Collins'] version of Joni Mitchell's 'Chelsea Morning.' We agreed on the spot that if we ever had a daughter we'd call her Chelsea."[27]

When they returned from their vacation, Bill announced that Hillary would be the chairperson of the Rural Health Advisory Committee. The purpose of the committee was to deal with the problems of providing health care to some of the state's most

Preparing Chelsea for the Spotlight

When *Newsweek* interviewed Hillary in 1992, they asked her how she and her husband prepared their young daughter for life in the spotlight of political campaigns:

> We've talked to her ever since she was about 6 or 7 years old about campaigns and the kind of things people say.... I knew that Chelsea by that time was old enough to turn on the TV and pay attention. And we were at dinner one night and I told her your daddy is going to run for governor again, and when people run for office, other people say things about them. And her eyes got real big—she just couldn't imagine that—and I said, you just pretend to be your daddy and what would you say if you want to run for governor. And she said something like, 'I've done a good job—elect me.'

Eleanor Clift, "I Think We're Ready," *Newsweek*, February 3, 1992, pp. 22–23.

isolated rural areas. The job was difficult but extremely rewarding for the lawyer who so much wanted to help provide for the needs of children and families. The experience on the committee would also prove valuable later in her career.

1980 was a bittersweet year for the Clintons. Before the new decade even began the couple had exciting news. According to Hillary:

> Bill and I had wanted to start a family immediately after we married, in 1975, but we were not having much luck. In 1979, we scheduled an appointment to visit a fertility clinic right after a long-awaited vacation. Lo and behold, I got pregnant. I have often remarked to my husband that we might have had more children if we had taken more vacations![28]

Chelsea Victoria Clinton was born on February 27, 1980. The birth announcement stated the parents' names as Bill Clinton and Hillary Rodham. Because Hillary had retained her maiden name, political adversaries took advantage of this fact to infer their relationship was more of a professional arrangement than a real

On February 27, 1980, Hillary and Bill Clinton celebrated the birth of their daughter, Chelsea Victoria.

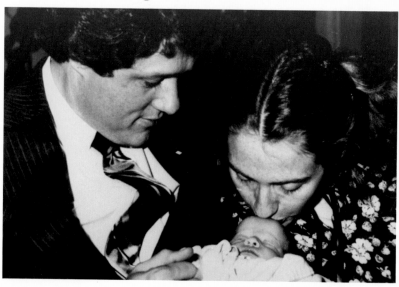

marriage. As far as Bill was concerned Hillary could choose any name she wanted but his advisors wanted her to legally change her name.

Other factors came into play when Bill ran for reelection. President Carter had allowed Cuban refugees into the United States and one of the places they were encamped was Fort Chaffee, Arkansas. The refugees rioted, forcing Clinton to call in the National Guard. During his first term Clinton also raised the registration fee for vehicles to help offset some of the state's economic problems. Clinton's opponents succeeded in convincing angry voters that the refugees and higher fees were the governor's fault. In November 1980, both President Carter and Governor Bill Clinton were voted out of office after one term.

Hillary Rodham Clinton

Bill Clinton fell into a despair which his wife tried to console as best as she could. There was only so much she could do since she was now a new mother and her years advocating for children were put to the ultimate test. As she later said:

> When Chelsea Victoria Clinton lay in my arms for the first time, I was overwhelmed by the love and responsibility I felt for her. Despite all the books I had read, all the children I had studied and advocated for, nothing had prepared me for the sheer miracle of her being.[29]

Bill and Hillary both decided that raising Chelsea was the most important thing to consider in whatever decision they made. Hillary made sure after she returned to work that Chelsea would end each day in her mother's company and she and Bill would coordinate their schedules according to their daughter's needs. They also decided that no matter what, Chelsea would never be affected by the demands of public scrutiny. They created for Chelsea what they called a "zone of privacy," in which the media would never be able to interview or intrude on Chelsea's life. Over the years, in spite of many attempts by the media to undermine it, the zone of privacy exists to this day.

Hillary's caseload at her law firm remained impressive while Bill took a position with another law firm in Arkansas. His despair over forced retirement from politics was short-lived as he immediately began planning his run for reelection in 1982. The controversy over his wife's name and appearance was bound to come up again. "The pressure on me to conform had increased dramatically when Bill was elected Governor in 1978," said Hillary. "For the first time I came to realize how my personal choices could impact my husband's political future ... I learned the hard way that some voters in Arkansas were seriously offended by the fact that I kept my maiden name."[30]

After much consideration, Hillary lost fifteen pounds, dyed her hair a lighter color, adjusted her wardrobe and legally changed her name to Hillary Rodham Clinton, all to help her husband regain the governership of Arkansas. The campaign was hard work for all concerned but the Clintons' teamwork paid off with Bill being sworn-in as governor in January of 1983.

Working First Lady

Hillary gave in to the demand to change her outward appearance and legal name but she would not compromise her core beliefs. During Bill's first term he made Hillary responsible for successfully raising the standard of medical care in the state—especially in the poorest rural areas—by creating a helicopter service called Angel One. She greatly diminished the state's infant mortality rate by creating the state's first neonatal care unit, and other successful programs.

Shortly after Bill returned to office, he named Hillary to head the Arkansas Education Standards Committee. It was formed to raise Arkansas' education ranking in the nation. Due to her love of children, he felt she would be perfect to improve the state's education system. Knowing the criticism she would again endure in taking such a position as the wife of the governor, Hillary reluctantly agreed to the job.

Hillary learned from her own parents and her work with children at Yale that one of the most important aspects of success in

As head of the Arkansas Education Standards Committee, Rodham Clinton expanded programs that helped prepare children for school by teaching parents how to get their children to read and write at home.

school was early childhood education. Children whose parents talked and read to them as early as possible had the highest level of success in school. Hillary discovered on the campaign trail that this was sadly lacking in Arkansas. She said:

> Chelsea was holding my hand when I approached a group of women and children and introduced myself. I said to one mother who was holding an infant, 'I bet you're having fun playing with her and talking to her all the time.' The woman looked at me in amazement and said, 'Why would I talk to her? She can't talk back.'[31]

This moment, and others like it, inspired Hillary to help expand the Home Instruction Program for Preschool Youngsters (HIPPY) throughout the state. The program prepared children for school before they started by teaching parents how to get their children to read and write at home. Over time, it proved to be so successful that Hillary was named Arkansas Woman of the Year by the state's press association in 1983.

Hillary's hard work in promoting the causes closest to her heart was not without controversy. Many people in Arkansas felt the job of a first lady was ceremonial and should consist of public appearances by her husband's side. Hillary may have changed her appearance, but working on the issues she felt should be a priority remained as important and unchanged to her as when she was a teenager inspired by Rev. Jones. When local press chose to write about her hairstyles instead of the state's educational crisis, Hillary reacted in character. She said, "Good grief, show me a woman who hasn't changed her hair! ... We really miss the boat when we don't pay attention to what's really going to change our children's lives and instead pay attention to my headbands."[32]

Controversy and Challenge

The most controversial aspect of Hillary's educational reforms regarded Arkansas' teachers. Hillary had traversed the state talking to involved individuals and worked tirelessly researching the best way to improve the education system. Although her support of a pay raise for teachers was welcomed, mandatory testing of all teachers was a major aspect of Hillary's plan that angered many educators.

Since Hillary saw the success in standardized tests for students, she felt the same should be expected of their teachers. At several public debates over the issue, Hillary was subjected to many personal attacks. "The debate was so bitter," she recalled, "one school librarian said I was 'lower than a snake's belly.' I tried to remember that I was being called names not because of who I was but what I represented."[33]

Hillary's education reforms were difficult to enact but they all dramatically enhanced student success throughout the state. President Reagan's Secretary of Education Terrence Bell publicly cited the reforms as being a role model for the whole country. She succeeded at these difficult tasks while still working as a lawyer and sitting on the boards for several large corporations such as Wal-Mart and the yogurt company TCBY.

As a board member she sought to enhance the role of women in the workplace. She also fought for it in her own profession as a member of the American Bar Association's Commission on Women in the Profession. She also continued her work with the Children's Defense Fund, becoming the chairperson in 1986 and flying to Washington monthly to organize the staff. Her work was rewarded with not only important improvements in Arkansas' way of life, but in 1988 and again in 1992 the National Law Journal named her one of the country's top 100 lawyers.

Race To The White House

All of Hillary's hard work helped her husband get reelected in 1984, 1986, 1988 and 1990. Her belief in her husband's agenda required her to defend him in sometimes unconventional ways. When Bill was in Washington on business during the election of 1990, his opponent Tom McRae held a press conference to deride the governor for not debating him and to degrade his record.

Democratic presidential hopeful Bill Clinton hugs Hillary at his election night party in February 1992. Controversy and accusations made the campaign difficult for the couple but they persevered and Bill won the election.

He did not mention that Clinton had challenged him to a debate to which McRae failed to appear. He also did not expect the governor's wife to show up at the press conference to state, "Tom, who was the one person who didn't show up at Springdale? Give me a break! I mean, I think we ought to get the record straight…"[34] She then embarrassed McRae by proudly listing many of her husband's impressive accomplishments.

Bill Clinton's tenure as governor began receiving national attention among Democratic Party officials. They approached him to run for president in 1988 but after much soul-searching, Bill and Hillary decided that Chelsea was still too young to be put through such intense scrutiny. By 1991 when Chelsea was eleven, they decided the time was right to take their message of a new form of political action to the national level.

The presidential race of 1992 was a battleground during the primary season with Bill and Hillary both defending themselves against accusations of marital unfaithfulness, lack of character and various other charges that emerged throughout the race. There was not much they endured that they had not experienced in Arkansas, but the national press corps and Bill's opponents were much more plentiful in the whole country. Bill Clinton overcame the obstacles, earned his party's nomination and ran for president against sitting Republican President George H. W. Bush and independent candidate Ross Perot in the general election.

Although there were moments when she was caught unprepared and some of her statements were taken out of context, Hillary Clinton's presence during the race was a very important aspect to her husband's growing popularity. According to Bill Clinton's campaign strategist George Stephanopoulos, "She was an unqualified political asset—her husband's chief adviser and candidate in her own parallel campaign… The fact that Clinton was with such a strong, smart, successful woman made people like him even more."[35]

On Election Day 1992, Bill Clinton was voted into the most powerful office of the free world. The innovative team of Bill and Hillary Rodham Clinton were poised for even higher levels of success and even greater public scrutiny as 42nd President and First Lady of the United States.

Highlights of Hillary on the Campaign Trail

Hillary proved to be a very important asset to her husband's presidential campaign. Here are a few examples:

George Stephanopoulos explains how their War Room Strategy came about early in the campaign: "The Republicans . . . had won three presidential campaigns in a row, and they were ruthless. We had to be battle ready just to be in the game—to break down the bureaucracy and replacing campaigning by conference call with a single strategic center for attacks and counterattacks. Hillary got it immediately. 'What you're describing is a war room,' she said, giving us both a name and an attitude."

George Stephanopoulos, *All Too Human: A Political Education*. New York: Little, Brown, 1999, p. 86.

When the campaign was in trouble, Hillary was often brought in to control the damage. Both Clintons appeared on the TV show *60 Minutes* to dismiss an early scandal. Hillary's words made her a national celebrity: "I'm not sitting here, some little woman standing by her man like [country singer] Tammy Wynette. I'm sitting here because I love him and I respect him and I honor what he's been through and what we've been through together. You know, if that's not enough for people then heck, don't vote for him."

Frontline: The Clinton Years, PBS Home Video, 2001.

Other times her words would have the opposite effect. When asked why she kept working during the campaign, Hillary made this off-the-cuff remark, which offended some voters when taken out of context: "I suppose I could have stayed home and baked cookies and had teas, but what I decided to do was to fulfill my profession which I entered before my husband entered public life."

Frontline: The Clinton Years, PBS Home Video, 2001.

Chapter 4

Hillaryland

Bill and Hillary Clinton became the first couple born after World War II to reside in the White House, radically altering the image most people had of the First Couple. Hillary continued to challenge the perception some people held of a modern woman. She also learned some hard lessons concerning how business is done in Washington by taking on the most far reaching social policy change in U.S. history.

A First Lady Like No Other

After Bill Clinton was elected, Hillary Clinton proved to be one of his most important aides during this chaotic stage. He had to find people for his cabinet and staff to help with the national economy, left in shambles by the previous administration. The problems with the economy resulted in a massive federal budget deficit that was the highest in history. This was an important priority, as were many of the other issues Clinton campaigned on that helped get him elected.

The process was chaotic but the outcome was historic. In her book about presidential marriages entitled *Hidden Power*, author Kati Marton wrote:

> By insisting that half of all senior political appointees be women, Hillary transformed the Washington political culture. It was her most enduring contribution. The women who ultimately headed up the Justice Department, Health and Human Services, Energy.... all owed Hillary a tremendous debt.[36]

First Lady Hillary Rodham Clinton stands in the East Room of the White House. She often advised her husband on political matters.

Hillary's advice to the new president was not new to their relationship. However, it was new and sometimes shocking to many people, in their concept of the president and first lady. She was not only a working first lady she was the only one in history with a postgraduate degree.

Hillary antagonized the media by requesting that the press corps no longer have offices inside the White House. They were moved elsewhere on the grounds of the White House, which increased the ongoing conflict between the first lady and the press corps. Although the criticism sometimes found Hillary questioning her ability, her husband felt she was more than up to the task. He later wrote:

Hillary would be the most professionally accomplished first lady in history. … Of course, such activism would make her more controversial with those who thought first ladies should stay above the fray, or who had disagreed with us politically, but that too, was part of what our generational change meant.[37]

A New Navigator

To prove his point of Hillary's worthiness, five days after Bill Clinton was sworn-in he named his wife to head the task force responsible for reforming health care. It was viewed as the most sweeping social change in America's history and had been attempted by almost every President of the twentieth century without success.

The nation's health care system was in serious need of overhaul for a multitude of reasons. Tens of millions of Americans either did not have enough health care coverage or in many cases had none at all due to the expensive cost. The system as it existed was draining the national economy and affecting America's ability to compete in the global market. Dealing with the problem quickly could greatly benefit the ailing economy and the average citizen.

The President boasted of his choice of Hillary chairing the board of the Health Care Task Force when he made his State of the Union Address later that year: "When I launched our nation

President Clinton appointed Hillary as the chair of the Health Care Task Force, which aimed to make the existing health care system better and increase access to health care for millions of Americans.

on this journey to reform the health care system, I knew I needed a talented navigator. Someone with a rigorous mind, a steady compass, a caring heart. Luckily, for me and our nation, I didn't have to look very far."[38]

Hillary Clinton wasted no time navigating the journey, having already set up an office and staff in the West Wing of the White House and dubbing it Hillaryland. No first lady had ever had offices in the West Wing before and it was criticized since it is where official business is conducted. Despite her critics, Hillary and her staff diligently worked at researching and forming the new laws. The task itself had two goals: Reform the existing system so it would be more fair and help the over forty million Americans without health care get access to it. The process included many in-depth interviews with individuals in the health care industry, government experts, and people dealing with catastrophic events when their insurance underpaid their needs. "I have never seen an issue that is as complicated as this," said Hillary at the time. "I can see why for fifty years people have tiptoed toward this problem and turned around and run away."[39]

Hard Work and Hard Times

The hard work Hillary and her staff were putting into the health care issue was made even more difficult by some of her early decisions made in the process as well as circumstances out of Hillary's control. Hillary decided to conduct all of her meetings in closed-door sessions that further alienated the media as well as opponents of the President's administration. Her decision was based on the one hundred days the president gave her to come up with the landmark legislation so it would be ready for the next session of congress. She thought the process would go faster without involving the media. This decision made Hillary even less popular among some important people in Washington.

In the midst of the intense long hours spent researching and organizing health care reform legislation, Hillary learned her father Hugh Rodham had suffered a massive stroke on March 1, 1993.

She rushed to his hospital bed with the rest of her family and kept a regular vigil. The family decided to take Hugh off of life support so that he could die peacefully but he surprised all by breathing on his own. It was not widely known that Hillary was struggling with fixing the health care crisis in America while dealing with a personal health care crisis of her own.

In early April, Hillary was scheduled to give a speech in Texas that forced her to leave her father's bedside to comment on the next millennium. She said in part:

> We need a new politics of meaning. ... We need a definition of civil society which answers the unanswerable questions posed by both market forces and the governmental ones, as to how we can have a society that fills up again and makes us feel that we are part of something bigger than ourselves.[40]

Her father passed away the next day.

In July the Clintons received more devastating news. Vince Foster, who had worked with Hillary at the Rose Law Firm and been a close family friend of the Clintons for many years, was found dead on a park bench with a gunshot wound to the head, the victim of an apparent suicide. Foster had been a legal advisor to the President and found the task to be more than he could handle when trying to fend off the accusations aimed at the first couple. A suicide note said: "I was not meant for the job or the spotlight of public life in Washington. Here ruining people is considered sport."[41]

The Clintons were emotionally distraught by the loss of their friend and colleague. Some of the media, already critical of the way the White House was being run, began insinuating that the Clintons may have had something to do with Foster's death. There were also ongoing media investigations of the Clintons' finances, personal relationship and Hillary's handling of the health care crisis. Journalist Bob Woodward observed, "Some confused her vigorous advocacy on behalf of certain points of view, especially on health care, with inflexibility. ..."[42]

The effect of such scrutiny was evident in the first lady's interviews at the time. When she was asked about the possible disaster that could come from her work on health care reform she later said,

> I understood, as many people never tired of telling me, that this could be a disaster, that I could get blamed. ... That didn't bother me. Heat comes with anything. If I had done nothing, I would have gotten heat. So better to get heat trying to do something important for people.[43]

The Talking Dog

The health care reform legislation was completed but the 1,200-page bill was severely criticized by opponents. Critics said it was too long, too complex and appeared to be a government takeover of the health care industry. Health insurance companies were the biggest opponents. They paid for a series of TV commercials with two actors as an elderly couple claiming that the new legislation would worsen the health care crisis in America.

To counter the negative publicity, Hillary went on a speaking tour around the country. Many experts in their field, such as

On September 28, 1993, Hillary Rodham Clinton became the first sitting first lady in history to testify before Congress to support her health care reform legislation.

former Surgeon General C. Everett Koop, found the legislation successful in addressing all the major issues of health care. As to its length, critics failed to mention that the majority of bills put before Congress are often longer than what the first lady was proposing. All of these points and more were mentioned on the first lady's speaking tour. Unfortunately, not many in the crowd got the message as hecklers shouted down Mrs. Clinton and threats of violence required the secret service to beef up security more than ever before.

On September 28, 1993, Hillary Clinton presented her case as the first sitting first lady in history to testify before Congress. Her testimony before the House Ways and Means Committee consisted of her opening statement and then answering questions put before her by the committee. Her knowledge and forthright delivery impressed almost everyone who witnessed it. Over the next several days she gave similar testimony in both the House and the Senate.

Hillary was grateful for the response but saw similarities to what she had dealt with from opponents in Arkansas. She said: "While many members genuinely appreciated the finer points of the health care debate, I realized that some of the laudatory responses to my testimony was just the latest example of 'the talking dog syndrome' which I had learned about as First Lady of Arkansas." She explained it as a quote evolved from 18th century writer Samuel Johnson who said, "A woman preaching is like a dog's walking on its hind legs. It is not done well, but you are surprised to find it done at all."[44]

Scandal After Scandal

The legislation finally presented to Congress on October 26th totaled 1,342 pages. Its presentation was battled on the senate floor with some Democrats complaining it was pro-industry while Republicans complained it was big government taking over the health care industry.

Later that night a weary Hillary Clinton climbed the stairs of the White House residence. Staff members gave her a hoopskirt and black wig to wear as Dolley Madison to her surprise birthday party. Then she was taken into her party where the staff of Hillaryland also wore outfits highlighting different aspects of Hillary's public image, from headbands to health care legislation. The President of the United States appeared in his own costume of white wig and tights. "Bill was disguised as President James Madison," said Hillary. "I loved him for it but I was glad we were living in the late twentieth century. He looks better in a suit."[45]

Because of political partisanship, the work of Hillary and her staff on health care reform resulted in the Health Security Act of 1994, a much weaker legislation. The bill that passed did not give health care coverage to the millions of Americans who needed it

The 'Gates' of Clinton

After the Watergate scandal during the Nixon Administration, journalists took to naming political scandals with the suffix *–gate*. There were several such scandals during the Clinton administration that directly or indirectly involved Hillary:

Troopergate: It was alleged that while governor of Arkansas, Bill Clinton used state troopers to bring women to his residence. The story was later discovered to be unfounded but hurt Hillary deeply.

Filegate: Accusations were made that Hillary took secret FBI files to find information to use against her enemies. Official investigations proved the story had no merit.

Travelgate: Hillary was accused of political spite when she oversaw the firing of several White House travel officers who had worked for the Bush administration. Investigation showed that Hillary had very little to do with the firings, and that the firings themselves were justified.

Gene Lyons and Joe Conason, *The Hunting of the President.* New York : Thomas Dunne Books, 2000.

nor did it improve the coverage for Americans who were under-insured. The Clinton Administration was greatly disappointed by the failure. It was then followed by the next elections in which the Republican Party took control of the Congress.

Following the failure of health care reform a series of unprecedented scandals rocked the White House, which drew focus away from the progressive reforms that the Clintons were attempting to enact. Millions were spent investigating the multiple scandals which eventually affected the administration's ability to govern. Each time, money and energy spent seeking to undermine the administration did not result in a single valid charge against the Clintons.

Woman Of The World

By early 1995, Hillary's role in her husband's administration appeared to be almost invisible. In truth, she was still as vital as before but chose a low profile by not appearing at staff meetings. She was being fully briefed on policy issues but discussed them at length with the President in private.

She also began a series of speaking engagements that took her around the world and bolstered her image and that of the United States in the international community. She traveled the world as an outspoken advocate of women and children's rights, earning a reputation as a speaker and goodwill ambassador that surpassed that of her childhood idol, First Lady Eleanor Roosevelt.

Of all her travels, the one that became the most famous was when she spoke in Beijing, China at the United Nations World Conference on Women. China had a long history of human rights violations and international events prior to the conference almost kept the first lady from appearing. The details of her visit were finalized and the American entourage, including Secretary of State Madeleine Albright, arrived in Beijing amid threats of unrest and violence.

Hillary took the stage and gave a speech equating the violation of women's rights with the violation of human rights. She

Rodham Clinton's first book, It Takes a Village, *was released in 1996 and became a bestseller. She donated the proceeds to children's charities.*

Hillary Clinton's Favorite First Lady

Of all the women who have been U.S. first lady, Hillary has often said her personal favorite was Eleanor Roosevelt. Roosevelt was a very public and controversial figure in her time. She often did legwork for President Franklin Delano Roosevelt, because his polio disease limited his mobility. After her husband died in office, Roosevelt continued to be a very public figure. In 1957 journalist Mike Wallace interviewed her, asking how it felt to be disliked by so many people:

Wallace: Mrs. Roosevelt, I think that you would agree that a good many people hated your husband. They even hated you.

Mrs. Roosevelt: Oh, yes. A great many still do.

Wallace: Why?

Mrs. Roosevelt: Well if you take a stand, in any way, and people feel that you have success in a following, those who disagree with you are going to feel strongly about it . . . There was a real core of hatred. The people would call him "that man." I remember one man who rejoiced, actually, when he died. But I suppose that this is just a feeling that certain people had that he was destroying the thing that they held dear and touched them. And naturally, you react to that with hatred.

Mike Wallace and Paul Gates, *Between You and Me.* New York: Hyperion, 2005, p. 38.

listed graphic examples of the abuse of women by individuals and governments. Albright recalled:

I didn't think it possible to arouse an audience in Beijing, which was made up of people from every culture listening to translators mangle the First Lady's grammar in a monotone. But Hillary's speech was a stunner. It was beautifully written and forcefully delivered… As the First Lady spoke, the multilingual chatter in the hall quieted. When she finished the applause came in waves.[46]

For Hillary's part, her new image as the most famous woman in the world was welcomed but the work was what mattered. She returned to the U.S. to discuss Beijing's conference on TV and radio call-in shows. One incident proved how much work was still needed: "I got a call from a man in the Middle East who asked me, what on earth did I mean that women's rights were human rights." And I said, 'Well, sir, if you would for a moment, shut your eyes and imagine all the rights that you, as a man, take for granted. We want the same rights.' And there was a pause. And he said, 'That's impossible!' Well it is not only not impossible, it must be made possible and real."[47]

Whitewater

1996 was another bittersweet year for the Clintons. Bill won reelection, becoming the first Democrat to do so since Franklin Roosevelt five decades earlier. Unfortunately, the Republicans still had control over both houses of Congress and opponents, led by House Speaker Newt Gingrich, stepped up the campaign to block the President's progressive policies.

Hillary wrote and published her first book that year entitled *It Takes A Village* which became a bestseller. She donated the proceeds to children's charities since the focus of the book concerned her most cherished subject. After recording an audio version of the book she also earned a Grammy Award for Best Spoken Word Recording.

Trying to promote the book proved difficult since most of the media preferred to ask her about the investigation into what was being called the Whitewater scandal. The scandal concerned some land in Arkansas the Clintons had purchased when Bill was governor. Although they lost money, the man they bought the land from, Jim McDougal, was under investigation. He was ultimately convicted for financial wrongdoing in another business venture and tried to bargain for a lesser charge by claiming to implicate the Clintons.

Although McDougal's efforts failed, the Clintons association with him was being investigated by the new Office of Independent Counsel (OIC) which was formed because of the Whitewater

Senator Christopher Bond holds a chart involving First Lady Hillary Rodham Clinton's Rose Law Firm billing records during a hearing of the Senate Whitewater Committee on May 8, 1996.

investigation. It began when Hillary refused to turn financial records over to a *Washington Post* reporter investigating the story. She did not feel their personal finances was anyone else's concern, resulting in the OIC coming into existence and ordering her to turn over the records.

The man in charge of the OIC was Ken Starr, a lawyer who admitted to having ties to the Republican Party, a fact that angered Hillary for its appearance of bias. The lengthy investigation cost millions and was criticized for leaking its findings regularly to the press.

Another first for a first lady, Hillary was subpoenaed to testify before a grand jury which questioned her possible mishandling of her financial records. She answered each question and found the entire experience was humiliating for her as she later told presidential advisor George Stephanopoulos. She said: "Whenever I go out and fight I get vilified, so I have just learned to smile and take it. I go out there and say 'Please, kick me again and insult me some more.' You have to be much craftier behind the scenes, but just smile."[48]

Monica Lewinsky

The Whitewater investigation continued but ultimately found no proof of wrongdoing. It eventually expanded its investigation to include other possible illegal activity of the Clinton administration. One example was the unsubstantiated rumor that had existed ever since Bill Clinton was governor that he had extramarital affairs and continued to do so even as President.

During his second term, a young White House intern named Monica Lewinsky made the accusations of the President's infidelities surface again. The President himself had testified under oath that he had not had an affair. Starr tried to utilize Lewinsky's statements secretly taped by a friend named Linda Tripp to prove the President had lied under oath. The pressure on Lewinsky, the President, his administration, and especially his family, intensified in the media and Washington in general.

Unlike the previous charges of infidelity, the Lewinsky scandal did not go away. When the pressure increased, the President admitted to the affair. Hillary was devastated by the admission and seriously considered a divorce. Ultimately, she turned again to spiritual advisors as she had done throughout her life. The problems in the relationship would be dealt with privately but publicly she would help her husband keep his job.

Impeachment

In December 1998, the House of Representatives voted to impeach the president. According to the U.S. Constitution articles of impeachment are voted on in the House and then if approved, go to the Senate for a vote to convict the President. Two articles were passed in the House charging the president with lying under oath and obstructing justice, both related to the Lewinsky affair.

Shortly after the Lewinsky story appeared in the media Hillary kept a previously scheduled appearance on the morning news

Hillary was devastated by her husband's affair but stood by him, in spite of increasingly personal and nasty newspaper headlines.

show *Today*. When asked about the accusations she said, "The great story here ... is the vast right-wing conspiracy that has been conspiring against my husband ..."[49] The phrase 'vast right-wing conspiracy' would often be used from then on by political opponents against Hillary. When opponents criticized the Clintons it was often couched in the statement that Hillary would claim the criticism was a result of a vast right-wing conspiracy.

The Senate argued for months over the impeachment charges until February 12, 1999. At that time, the vote was taken and the conviction against President Clinton failed to garner enough votes. Although impeached, his presidency was spared. The Clintons' marriage was also affected by the scandal as they considered first a divorce and then later a marriage counselor. During the scandal Hillary defended her husband but was no longer on speaking terms with him.

In The End

Not all of what Hillary Clinton experienced in her husband's second term was as demeaning. She still managed to play the role of American hostess to the world via the front gates of the White House and write two more bestselling books while her husband was in office. She also hosted the White House's first conference for childcare in 1997. She helped renovate the building known as America's house for the first time in fifty years and installed a state of the art White House Website for virtual tours and international conferencing.

One of the first lady's proudest achievements was in the preservation of America's past. She helped preserve and restore the original flag Francis Scott Key wrote about in The Star Spangled Banner as well as other important historical artifacts. She continued to advocate for children and was voted the most admired woman in America in several polls by the end of her husband's term.

As for her husband's legacy, the American people showed their admiration for him and his wife's work despite the scandals. He left office with the highest poll rating of any retiring president. This was due to the economy being the strongest in history, the budget going from a huge deficit to a big surplus, welfare being reformed, crime lowered, and the largest amount of land protected and preserved.

In spite of not enacting significant health care reform as well as her run-ins with the press and the various scandals, Hillary Rodham Clinton left the White House a stronger, more evolved public figure than she had entered it. Her lessons were learned and as the next election year approached, she would break again with tradition to test the limits of progressive thinking more than ever before.

Chapter 5

Casting Her Own Shadow

Stepping out from her husband's shadow, Hillary Clinton chose to cast her own shadow in the public spotlight. Taking the valuable lessons learned from her experiences in her husband's campaigns, she continued to improve her political knowledge, but this time she was the candidate.

Run Hillary, Run!

The positive poll numbers the Clintons received as they were leaving the White House did not last long. Just days before leaving the White House President Clinton authorized several executive pardons, such as controversial fugitive financier Marc Rich, wanted for tax evasion. The Clintons also left the White House with several gifts from supporters, such as rare artwork and a Mickey Mantle baseball card. They eventually returned the gifts because of public outcry from many who thought the Clintons had no right to keep gifts meant for the White House.

Before any of this took place, Hillary Rodham Clinton received an amazing offer while still First Lady. Democratic New York Senator Daniel Patrick Moynihan, who held the office for almost three decades, announced in 1998 that he would retire when his current term ended in 2001. The announcement sent the Democratic Party into a frenzy of activity as they searched for a candidate who would help them keep the long held position.

Possibilities included everyone from other local politicians in New York to high-profile individuals like John F. Kennedy, Jr.

While Bill Clinton's impeachment trial was going on in Congress, Hillary was approached by several Democratic Party leaders to run for the Senate in New York. They believed that the Republican candidate would be popular New York mayor Rudy Giuliani which meant they would need an equally well-known candidate to compete. On the day Bill Clinton was acquitted in Congress, Hillary watched the proceedings on TV while conducting a meeting with White House advisor Harold Ickes to discuss the pros and cons of running for senate in New York.

Almost all of Hillary's closest advisors tried to talk her out of it even though she and Bill had already decided they would retire in New York. They established their residency by buying a home in the Westchester New York suburb of Chappaqua. She however, continued to question whether to run for several more months. Her husband supported the idea of running by stating: "I am very grateful that now my wife has a chance to do what I thought she ought to do twenty-six years ago when we finished law school."[50]

Ultimately, her decision was spiritually-based, which had often been the case in Hillary Clinton's life. She received a letter from an Arkansas priest named Father George Tribou whom she had befriended years before. The letter said in part:

> It is my opinion that on Judgment Day the first question God asks is not about the Ten Commandments. … but what He asks each of us is this: WHAT DID YOU DO WITH THE TIME AND THE TALENTS I GAVE YOU?… Those who feel you are not up to handling the hostile New York press and the taunts of your opponents fail to realize that, having been tried in the fire, you can handle anything. Bottom line: run Hillary run! My prayers will be with you all the way.[51]

Making It Official

Beginning the next week, Hillary made several official announcements to confirm her candidacy for the New York Senate race. The

In 2000 Hillary Rodham Clinton announced her plans to run for the New York Senate race, citing the need for improved public education and health care.

first announcement took place on the grounds of Sen. Moynihan's upstate New York farm in the presence of Moynihan, his wife Liz, and countless members of the worldwide media.

In her announcement, she stated,

> Some people are asking why I'm doing this here and now. That's a fair question. Here's my answer—and why I hope you'll put me to work for you: I may be new to the neighborhood. But I'm not new to your concerns. … For over thirty years, in many different ways, I've seen firsthand the kind of challenges New Yorkers face today. I care about the same issues you do. I do understand them. I can make progress on them.[52]

Hillary's statement underscored what she knew she would be in for. Because she was from out-of-state, she knew some people would call her a carpetbagger, a criticism from the Post-Civil War era for Northerners who moved to the South to change the laws during Reconstruction. It has since been used just as negatively to describe a politician who establishes residency in an area to seek public office. Hillary addressed the issue of being a carpetbagger throughout the campaign by stating, "What I'm for is maybe as important, if not more important, than where I'm from."[53]

The Listening Tour

Her opponent did indeed turn out to be Mayor Giuliani. He wasted no time in referring to Hillary as a carpetbagger who knew nothing about the diverse and outspoken populace of New York. Hillary was advised by her campaign staff to spend as much time in New York City as possible so New Yorkers could get to know her better. She did campaign in New York City, often in the company of New York's other Senator, Democrat Chuck Schumer. However, against the advice of much of her staff, she chose to also campaign as much as possible in upstate New York.

A sign protests a campaign appearance by Hillary in upstate New York. Largely conservative, upstate New York was considered a waste of time by Clinton's advisors, but eventually helped win her the race.

Largely conservative, upstate was considered a waste of time by her advisors. Hillary chose to campaign in the region with what she called The Listening Tour, where she would meet with small groups of local citizens and talk with them about what was important in their lives. The kickoff event was in Westchester County, where she promised to visit all 62 counties in the state of New York, which no candidate had ever done before. She reminded the crowd that it would be a brutal campaign with rehashes of scandals from the past eight years. She closed by adding in a purposely fake New York accent, "I know it's not going to be an easy campaign, but hey, dis is New Yawk."[54]

When The Listening Tour began, Hillary was way behind in the polls. There were also several statements and events that early on had a negative effect. One example was that as First Lady she was required to meet and greet many famous dignitaries. When she met Suha Arafat, the wife of Palestinian Liberation Organization leader Yasir Arafat, she was photographed kissing her as a matter of protocol. This did not sit well with many of the Jewish voters in New York who considered Arafat a terrorist who wanted to abolish the Jewish state of Israel. Early in the campaign, Hillary found herself apologizing or defending much of what she did.

A Whole New Race

As The Listening Tour progressed and Hillary's campaign skills improved, the polls began to show a seesaw effect. One day Hillary would be up a few points, the next day Giuliani would be slightly ahead. The polls were also showing the same effect in the Republican stronghold of upstate as Hillary kept her promise to visit every county in New York.

The campaign was in full swing when Rudy Giuliani surprised his supporters by dropping out of the race in May, 2000. The reason he gave was that he was fighting against prostate cancer but it also became publicly known that his wife was divorcing him in what amounted to another public scandal. Hillary chose not to comment on the events in Giuliani's life and wished him a speedy recovery.

Giuliani's replacement was a fairly young, very competitive Long Island congressman named Rick Lazio. He launched his campaign with a letter writing campaign to other Republican voters to raise money. He wrote, "It won't take me six pages to convince you to send me an urgently needed contribution for my United States Senate campaign in New York. It would only take six words. I'm running against Hillary Rodham Clinton."[55] So disliked was Hillary by the Republicans, Lazio received over forty million dollars in donations from around the country.

Not to be outdone, Hillary responded immediately to Lazio's letter-writing campaign. She said, "My opponent says you only need to know six words about him: 'I'm running against Hillary Rodham Clinton.' Well, I think you need to know seven words to vote for me. How about *jobs, education, environment, choice, health and Social Security?*"[56]

The two candidates debated each other three times during the campaign. At one point during the first debate, Lazio walked over

Hillary Rodham Clinton and opponent Rick Lazio debated each other three times during the New York Senate race.

to Hillary's podium and asked her to sign a statement concerning campaign contributions. He assumed that by getting into Hillary's physical space he would shake up her demeanor. Hillary kept her cool until Lazio returned to his own podium on the other side of the stage.

The next day, the overnight polls showed Lazio's aggressive act made him seem like a bully and hurt his campaign with Hillary scoring much higher numbers than before. Lazio was much more subdued in the other debates but the damage to his campaign was done. When Hillary was asked if she wanted to punch Lazio in the nose during the first debate, she brushed off the question and said, "The thing that probably prepared me best in dealing with things like that was having two younger brothers."[57]

Election Night

Hillary campaigned vigorously in New York throughout the rest of the year while still maintaining her necessary duties as First Lady. These included organizing and hosting a massive reception at the White House for the fiftieth anniversary of NATO, the organization of national governments teamed together to promote democracy in the world after World War II. The details of such an event were tremendous since every major world leader would be in attendance and proper protocol had to be followed precisely. She also hosted several major events to usher in the new millennium.

Hillary showed stamina and continued her double duty as the nation's First Lady and New York's Democratic Senatorial candidate. On Election night November 2000, Hillary and her staff thought she might barely be able to win the race. When the results came in, she won by much larger numbers then anyone had predicted, which included a big win in the upstate New York counties that usually vote Republican. Her strategy paid off. By campaigning upstate and remaining focused on the issues that mattered to New Yorkers, she became the state's first female senator.

She accepted the outcome graciously and with good humor by stating to her supporters,

Sixty-two counties, sixteen months, three debates, two opponents, and six black pantsuits later, because of you, we are here. You came out and said issues and ideals matter. Jobs matter, downstate and upstate. The environment matters. Social Security matters. A woman's right to choose matters. It all matters, and I just want to say, from the bottom of my heart, thank you, New York.[58]

The Junior Senator from New York

Hillary was sworn-in on January 3, 2001 and for the next seventeen days she was senator and first lady at the same time. She and her husband were back on speaking terms by the time she was sworn-in and were getting along better than they had for some time. Bill let it be known how he felt watching Vice-President Al Gore administer the oath of office to Hillary. Clinton said, "I was so excited I almost jumped over the railing."[59]

Senator Clinton become the first New York Senator to become chair of the Senate's powerful Armed Services Committee. Here, she talks with Army Surgeon General Kevin Kiley on Capitol Hill.

After her orientation period she proceeded to keep a low-profile in the Senate but built important relationships with Democratic and Republican Senators alike. She again made history when she was named the chair of the Senate's powerful Armed Services Committee, responsible for the oversight of the military. She was the first New York senator to ever hold that position.

Hillary also wasted no time in fulfilling her promise to New Yorkers. She fought to get tax breaks for businesses that would move to her state and although it took time to succeed, the unemployment rate in upstate New York dropped considerably. She also led a bipartisan effort to bring broadband internet access to rural communities.

When asked during her first year in office how she felt about choosing public service, her answer was philosophical. She said in part:

> Choosing public service is a very personal decision and no one can make it for you. You have to look deep inside yourself and examine your motives, and think hard about what you would do to make a difference. Then you have to be willing to subject yourself to a very tough and sometimes mean-spirited political environment. But I can tell you, from the heart, it's worth it.[60]

September 11, 2001

In the morning hours of September 11, two passenger jet airliners were forced by terrorists to crash into the towers of the World Trade Center, causing the worst civilian attack in American history. There were two other such tragedies moments apart and when the smoke cleared, thousands of people were dead.

Although only nine months into her term as New York's senator, Hillary Clinton was deeply involved in helping the relief effort. Along with fellow Senator Schumer, she successfully lobbied Congress for federal aid and secured over 21 billion dollars to fund the destroyed World Trade Center's site. She also issued two studies involving the 9/11 tragedy. One examined the disbursement of funds to local communities and the other explored the effects of the crisis on the survivors, families and emergency workers who responded during and after the tragedy. On the Armed Services Committee she supported military action in Afghanistan in the belief that Osama Bin Laden, the man thought to be responsible for September 11, could be found there.

In spite of her hard work to help New York deal with the tragedy, Hillary still encountered negative feedback. At an all-star concert held at New York's Madison Square Garden to honor the police, fire and emergency workers who heroically sacrificed themselves, audience members soundly booed Hillary when she took the stage. They may not have been aware of the work she was doing on their behalf in the Senate as she was less high-profile than Mayor Giuliani who was applauded by the crowd. Whatever the reason, Hillary raised her voice above the noise, introduced the next act and quickly left the stage.

The Senate's Rising Star

Various legislation and committee appointments kept her active and productive throughout her term, winning her a begrudging respect from former opponents of her husband's administration. In 2005 she worked with Clinton Administration opponent and former Speaker of the House Newt Gingrich to propose eventual universal health care. Another Republican, Majority Leader Bill Frist, worked with Hillary to legislate the updating of hospital records to computers, in order to ease the burden and cost on patients and hospital staff.

Although her attempt to reform health care failed as First Lady, it was still a priority for her as Senator. "All that we have learned in the last decade confirms that our goal should continue to be what every other industrialized nation has achieved," she said, "health care that's always there for every citizen."[61]

By 2006 she easily won reelection with one of the largest majorities in New York history. She had become one of the most high profile and accessible members of the U.S. Senate. She continued to work consistently for the rights of families, children and working parents, as well as incremental improvements in the health care system whenever possible.

In spite of her improved reputation in working with opposing senators, her greatest struggles in the Senate were fought against the administration of President Bush. She challenged his policies whenever possible since many of the changes her husband enacted as president were being overturned by Bush. She was frustrated by a lack a success since the Republicans held the majority in the Senate and she could not rally enough votes to overturn his decisions.

Following the Democratic Party's defeat in presidential elections of 2000 and 2004, Party leaders approached her to run in the next presidential election. She gave it serious soul-searching consideration and prepared to make her decision by January 2007.

Chapter 6

Race For The White House

With even greater lessons learned from previous campaigns, Hillary Clinton decided to run for President in 2008. It was the culmination of a life spent breaking down barriers and challenging preconceptions. She would utilize this experience in a race that was like no other in the history of American politics.

A Race Like No Other

Almost all presidential elections are unique in their own way but the presidential race of 2008 has many firsts for American politics. It is the first presidential race in 80 years in which neither a sitting president or his vice-president is seeking the office, leaving the choice completely wide open. This was one of several reasons that led Hillary to her decision to break new ground in her run for the White House as a presidential candidate.

The race for the White House has now become more electronically sophisticated than ever before. In the past, candidates had campaigned and raised funds via such venues as train stop campaigns and television ads. For the first time, all the declared candidates have set up internet websites for regular webcasts, issue-related blogs and fundraising efforts. Hillary utilized the new technology to make her announcement official.

It is also the first time the perceived frontrunners of both the Republican and Democratic parties look more different than

The presidential race of 2008 was the first time all the declared candidates set up Internet Web sites for blogs and fundraising efforts.

ever before. In the past, presidential candidates had usually been white, middle-aged, Protestant men. The Constitution states that a candidate need only be at least 35-years of age and born in the United States. Cultural and social requirements have been much tougher but even that appears to be dramatically shifting. Some of the major declared candidates include such Republicans as Mitt Romney, a Mormon, and Hillary's original New York Senate opponent, Rudy Giuliani, a Catholic. The Democratic candidates are even more diverse with Hispanic New Mexico Governor Bill Richardson, 45-year-old African-American Barack Obama and the widely perceived frontrunner of the party, female candidate Hillary Rodham Clinton.

In It To Win

On January 20, 2007, following much predicting and guesswork by both major parties and political strategists, Hillary Clinton made it official. She launched a website called Hillaryclinton.com

Pioneering Women Politicians

Newsweek presented a timeline of female politicians who laid the groundwork for women in the political arena:

Elizabeth Cady Stanton (1866): The first woman to run for the House of Representatives. Although she was not eligible to vote [until 1920], she received 24 out of 12,000 votes as an independent from New York.

Victoria Woodhull (1872): She was the first woman nominated as a presidential candidate (on the Equal Rights Party ticket).

Jeannette Rankin (1917): Represented Montana's Second District and was the first woman to serve in either chamber of Congress. Only lawmaker to vote against U.S. entry into both World Wars.

Hattie Wyatt Caraway (1932): Appointed a senator after the death of her husband in late 1931. She ran for the seat in 1932 and became the first woman elected to the Senate, serving two terms.

Margaret Chase Smith (1964): The first woman to have her name placed in nomination for president at a major party convention and to serve in both houses of Congress.

Shirley Chisholm (1968): The first African American woman elected to Congress, she served New York's Twelfth District. In '72 she became the first black to seek the presidency.

Geraldine Ferraro (1984): The first female Democratic vice presidential nominee when chosen by presidential candidate Walter Mondale.

Carol Moseley Braun (1992): The Illinois native defeated the incumbent in the Democratic primary and won the general election to become the first African American woman in the U.S. Senate.

Nancy Pelosi (2007): California's Eighth District representative was voted by Congress to become the first female speaker of the House.

Newsweek, 12/25/06–1/1/07, pp. 30–40.

Some analysts in the media believed the release of Clinton's book Living History *in 2003 was a way of testing reactions to a possible run for president.*

and said of the 2008 presidential election, "I'm in it to win. And that's what I intend to do."[62]

Her historic announcement was not entirely unexpected but it was years in the making. As early as 2003 there was talk of her possibly running for president when her autobiography *Living History* was published and became a national bestseller. Some analysts in the media believed Hillary was testing reactions to her possible announcement and the book was one way of doing just that.

The presidential race of 2004 went on without her but it was a controversial race just the same. In 2000 the Supreme Court had decided the race when problems arose from the ballots in Florida resulting in Republican candidate George W. Bush winning the electoral vote in Court but Democrat Al Gore winning the popular vote. The controversy continued four years later when polls in Ohio were also in question. President Bush won reelection and the Democratic candidate John Kerry accused his opponent of unfair practices. Kerry's Vietnam War record as a swiftboat commander had been questioned by the Bush campaign. Bush's campaign did so indirectly by launching a series of ads of other swiftboat veterans who criticized Kerry's record. Kerry complained about the ads after the fact and this subtle act created the term "swiftboating" for national political hijinks that ultimately succeeded.

Democratic party leaders were looking for a winning candidate and the two front-runners were Illinois Senator Barack Obama and New York Senator Hillary Clinton, pictured here during the first Democratic presidential primary debate.

Hillary's Presidential Campaign Manager

Hillary's campaign manager was named a 2007 Woman of Distinction by *Hispanic Magazine* in the following profile:

Patti Solis Doyle has earned a reputation in Washington as an adept fundraiser and effective Strategist. As campaign manager for Hillary Clinton for president, she is the first Hispanic woman to lead a bid for the White House.

A longtime Clinton collaborator, Doyle met Sen. Clinton nearly sixteen years ago, when she became her chief scheduler in Arkansas. When the Clintons moved into the White House, Doyle came too, working as director of scheduling and advance for the first lady and later as an Assistant to President of the United States. She went to work for Sen. Clinton's 2000 election campaign becoming one of her most trusted advisors.

Hillary Clinton's campaign manager Patti Solis Doyle.

In addition to generating campaign donations and developing the next move with Sen. Clinton, Doyle is behind the expensive but potentially risky financial strategy that has made Sen. Clinton one of the top fundraisers on the campaign trail.

Idy Fernandez, "Latinas of Excellence," *Hispanic Magazine*, May 2007.

http://hol.hispaniconline.com/ HispanicMag/2007_5

Although she was not a candidate, there was much swiftboating of Hillary in 2004 and beyond. Conservative commentators that continued to berate and ridicule Hillary in public published several books. The accusations ranged from calling her a power hungry opportunist to a wife who remained married strictly to advance her political career. Much of what was written about her proved to be inconsequential while some of it showed the real reasons her opponents tried to demonize her. Former Ronald Reagan and George Bush Sr. speechwriter Peggy Noonan explained in part why conservatives should be worried if Hillary decided to run for president. She said, "Because Mrs. Clinton is smarter than her husband and has become a better campaigner ... she has found a way to grow more emotionally mature."[63]

The Iraq War

The Presidential election of 2004 existed without Hillary Clinton in the race, due mainly to her work in the Senate. As she continued to fight mainly for the rights of New Yorkers—along with her ongoing goals of fighting for families and health care reform—events in the world and the way in which the Bush Administration dealt with them began to take more of her focus.

Following the 9/11 attacks President Bush sent troops into Afghanistan to bring down the Taliban. They were the regime in power that protected Osama Bin Laden but he was never found. As the president's war on terrorism continued, he asked Congress to authorize a similar invasion of Iraq to end the regime of dictator Saddam Hussein. Hillary Clinton voted to authorize the invasion, along with a majority of her colleagues, based on the President's varied reasons. Those reasons included Hussein's boasting of having weapons of mass destruction and a possible link to Bin Laden's Al Qaeda organization.

Over time, those reasons came into question as the war in Iraq continued. Hillary herself went to Afghanistan and Iraq several times to see the progress being made. She returned with questions for the Bush Administration that remained unanswered as American citizens also became more disenchanted with the war. The questions ranged from what the administration's plans were for getting American troops out of Iraq to whether or not the new government of Iraq was prepared to defend itself against insurgents. As the war dragged on it became the single most talked about issue of the presidential race.

Other candidates denounced or apologized for their vote authorizing the war, such as former Senator John Edwards and Senators Joe Biden and Chris Dodd. Hillary again drew criticism for not doing the same. She said, "Knowing what I know now, I would never have voted for it. The President was the one who was wrong. The President led people to believe that he would be prudent in the exercise of the authority he was given. That proved not to be true."[64]

Conflict with the Bush Administration

It was the fact that Hillary had several such conflicts with the Bush Administration that led her to her decision to run for president. The federal budget surplus that her husband's administration had created was gone and the deficit in the budget had returned and grown during the Bush Administration.

Either the President or other members of the Republican Party in the Congress defeated the incremental changes in health care she worked for as Senator. Horror stories from her constituents continued to flood Hillary's senate office. Senior citizens could not get their prescriptions filled because they were confused by the changes in the President's Medicare drug coverage plan. Hillary helped the constituents as best as she could, knowing a better national health care system was desperately needed. This and other factors made health care reform the most important issue in the race after the Iraq War. Many of the candidates, including Hillary, have stated this was a major factor in their candidacy.

The other Democrats in the race unveiled their health care plans. They included raising taxes to pay for universal health insurance or other plans that were similar to either Canada's plan or Hillary's plan from 1993.

Senator Clinton stated that failures in the health care system by the Bush administration was a major factor in her candidacy.

She spotlighted the consensus of opinion she lacked in 1993, but was present during the 2008 race. She said,

> I have the scars to show for that experience. But I am convinced that now, when the Democrats all are coming forward saying this has to be a national goal, we then can try to get the political will… What's important and what I learned in the previous effort is you've got to have the political will —a broad coalition of business and labor, doctors, nurses, hospitals, everybody—standing firm when the inevitable attacks come from the insurance companies and the pharmaceutical

companies that don't want to change the system because they make so much money out of it.[65]

Other issues in the presidential race include the problem of global warming, the continuing risk of terrorist attacks in America, ending the country's dependence on foreign oil and the damage America's image has suffered in the international community since the Iraq War. Hillary has proposed specific plans to deal with these issues that in some cases differ slightly from her rivals but in other instances are extremely different. Overall, Hillary has said about the race, "I am worried about the future of our country and I want to help put it back on the right course, so that we can work together to meet the challenges that confront us at home and abroad … I believe I am in the best position to be able to do that."[66]

Hairstyles and Hemlines

Hillary Clinton's position in the race as an early frontrunner has led many major newspapers and magazines to raise the issue of her gender as a possible problem. She is fully aware of the unique aspect of her candidacy but has chosen to run on her record as her strength. The gender issue itself has been downplayed since it is a subject Hillary has dealt with her whole life with the simple idea that it will never be known if a woman can be president until it is at least tried.

Interestingly, one of the biggest obstacles to her campaign has been other women. Early polls have shown that most women are more critical of a female candidate then some men are. White House Project director Marie Wilson, which was set up to advance women candidates, has seen the problem first hand. She has said, "Too often when a woman runs, it's about being man enough for the job—and hair, hemline, and husband."[67]

Hillary's campaign has addressed the issue with targeted fundraisers for and by women that have shown her polls numbers among women steadily rising. The question of whether any woman, even Hillary Clinton, can do a job traditionally held by a man may finally be put to rest with the 2008 presidential election.

What it Takes To Win

The fundraising she accomplished from the beginning of her candidacy became a necessary part of the job. Hillary Clinton used her organizational skills to set up polls, raise a record amount of funding, and create a campaign team that is the envy of national politics. Many of her staff were involved in getting her husband elected while others, such as campaign manager Patti Solis Doyle, have been longtime members of Hillary's inner circle from Hillaryland.

Clinton broke fundraising records from the beginning of her candidacy with many campaign stops and speeches throughout the country.

Part of the reason for her intense early fight for a race that still has a way to go has to do with more changes in the process. Although traditionally the first primaries are held in Iowa and New Hampshire, several important states, such as New York, California, New Jersey and Nevada—to which Clinton has traveled and campaigned extensively—have moved their primaries closer to the beginning of the year. This has required all the major candidates to raise record amounts of money in a short period of time to compete on TV and other venues within the early primary states. The leader of each quarter's fundraising effort has consistently been Hillary Clinton.

Political analyst Susan Estrich has been involved in national politics since the early 1980s and feels Hillary is more than up to the task. She wrote a book entitled *The Case For Hillary Clinton* in response to Peggy Noonan's *The Case Against Hillary Clinton*. In it, Estrich wrote, "Since 1980 the candidates with the most money, the best organization—the ones who were supposed to win—have indeed won."[68]

Whatever the outcome of the 2008 presidential election, Hillary Rodham Clinton will continue to break down barriers by challenging the preconception of women's role in society and making the impossible possible.

Introduction: Making the Impossible Possible

1. Hillary Rodham Clinton, *Living History*. NY, NY: Simon & Schuster, 2003, p. 41.
2. Hillary Rodham Clinton, *It Takes A Village: And Other Lessons Children Teach Us*. NY, NY: Simon & Schuster, 1996, pp. 317–318.
3. Quoted in Carl Sferrazza Anthony, "What I Hope to Do as First Lady," *Good Housekeeping*, January, 1993, p. 99.
4. Quoted in Catherine Whitney, *Nine and Counting: The Women of the Senate*. New York: Harper Collins, 2001, p. 210.

Chapter 1: In Her Time

5. Quoted in Clinton, *Living History*. NY, NY: Simon & Schuster, 2003, p. 3.
6. Quoted in Gail Sheehy, "What Hillary Wants," *Vanity Fair*, May, 1992, p. 213.
7. Quoted in Anthony, "What I Hope to Do as First Lady," *Good Housekeeping*, January, 1993, p. 98.
8. Quoted in Kati Marton, *Hidden Power: Presidential Marriages That Shaped Our Recent History*. New York: Random House, 2001, p. 310.
9. Clinton, *Living History*. NY, NY: Simon & Schuster, 2003, p. 4.
10. Quoted in Howard G. Chua-Eoan, Nina Burleigh, Linda Kramer, "Power Mom," *People*, January 25, 1993, p. 58.
11. Clinton, *It Takes A Village: And Other Lessons Children Teach Us*. NY, NY: Simon & Schuster, 1996, pp. 9–10.
12. Clinton, *Living History*. NY, NY: Simon & Schuster, 2003, p. 22.
13. Quoted in Chua-Eoan, Burleigh, Kramer, "Power Mom," *People*, January 25, 1993, p. 58.
14. Clinton, *Living History*. NY, NY: Simon & Schuster, 2003, p. 18.

15. Clinton, "The Class of '69," *Life*, June 20, 1969, p. 31.
16. Clinton, *Living History*. NY, NY: Simon & Schuster, 2003, p. 40.

Chapter 2: "Billary"

17. Clinton, *Living History*. NY, NY: Simon & Schuster, 2003, p. 38.
18. Quoted in Bill Clinton, *My Life*. New York: Knopf, 2004, p. 181.
19. Clinton, *My Life*. New York: Knopf, 2004, p. 182.
20. Clinton, *My Life*. New York: Knopf, 2004, p. 182.
21. Quoted in Eleanor Clift, "I Think We're Ready," *Newsweek*, February 3, 1992, p. 21.
22. Clinton, *Living History*. NY, NY: Simon & Schuster, 2003, p. 71.
23. Quoted in Marton, *Hidden Power: Presidential Marriages That Shaped Our Recent History*. New York: Random House, 2001, p. 310.
24. Quoted in Clinton, *Living History*. NY, NY: Simon & Schuster, 2003, p. 74.
25. Clinton, *Living History*. NY, NY: Simon & Schuster, 2003, pp. 77–78.

Chapter 3: From State House To White House

26. Quoted in Elizabeth Sporkin, Margie Bonnett Sellinger, "Practical Chic," *People*, January 25, 1993, p. 58.
27. Clinton, *My Life*. New York: Knopf, 2004, p. 73.
28. Clinton, *It Takes A Village: And Other Lessons Children Teach Us*. NY, NY: Simon & Schuster, 1996, p. 8.
29. Clinton, *It Takes A Village: And Other Lessons Children Teach Us*. NY, NY: Simon & Schuster, 1996, p. 7.
30. Clinton, *Living History*. NY, NY: Simon & Schuster, 2003, p. 91.
31. Clinton, *It Takes A Village: And Other Lessons Children Teach Us*. NY, NY: Simon & Schuster, 1996, pp. 98–99.
32. Quoted in Anthony, "What I Hope to Do as First Lady," *Good Housekeeping*, January, 1993, p. 99.

33. Clinton, *Living History*. NY, NY: Simon & Schuster, 2003, p. 94.
34. Quoted in Gail Sheehy, "What Hillary Wants," *Vanity Fair*, May, 1992, p. 142.
35. George Stephanopoulos, *All Too Human: A Political Education*. New York: Little, Brown, 1999, pp. 91–92.

Chapter 4: Hillaryland

36. Marton, *Hidden Power: Presidential Marriages That Shaped Our Recent History*. New York: Random House, 2001, p. 319.
37. Clinton, *My Life*. New York: Knopf, 2004, p. 469.
38. Quoted in *Frontline: The Clinton Years*, PBS Home Video, 2001.
39. Quoted in Margaret Carlson Washington, "An Interview with Hillary Rodham Clinton: 'We've Had Some Good Times,'" Time, May 10, 1993. http://www.time.com/0, 8816,978433,00.html
40. Quoted in Clinton, *My Life*. New York: Knopf, 2004, p. 501.
41. Quoted in Clinton, *My Life*. New York: Knopf, 2004, p. 532.
42. Quoted in Bob Woodward, *The Agenda: Inside the Clinton White House*. New York: Simon & Schuster, 1994, p. 333.
43. Quoted in Marton, *Hidden Power: Presidential Marriages That Shaped Our Recent History*. New York: Random House, 2001, p. 322.
44. Clinton, *Living History*. NY, NY: Simon & Schuster, 2003, p. 190.
45. Clinton, *Living History*. NY, NY: Simon & Schuster, 2003, pp. 32–33.
46. Madeleine Albright, *Madame Secretary*, New York: Miramax Books, 2003, p. 198.
47. Quoted in Susan Estrich, *The Case For Hillary Clinton*. New York: Harper Collins, 2005, p. 216.
48. Quoted in Marton, *Hidden Power: Presidential Marriages That Shaped Our Recent History*. New York: Random House, 2001, p. 336.

49. Quoted in *Frontline: The Clinton Years*, PBS Home Video, 2001.

Chapter 5: Casting Her Own Shadow

50. Quoted in Marton, *Hidden Power: Presidential Marriages That Shaped Our Recent History*. New York: Random House, 2001, p. 346.
51. Quoted in Clinton, *Living History*. NY, NY: Simon & Schuster, 2003, pp. 505–506.
52. Quoted in Whitney, *Nine and Counting: The Women of the Senate*. New York: Harper Collins, 2001, p. 204.
53. Quoted in Beth J. Harpaz, *The Girls in the Van: Covering Hillary*. New York: St. Martins, 2001, p. 44.
54. Quoted in Patrick S. Halley, *On The Road with Hillary*. New York: Viking, 2002, p. 299.
55. Quoted in Whitney, *Nine and Counting: The Women of the Senate*. New York: Harper Collins, 2001, p. 204.
56. Quoted in Harpaz, *The Girls in the Van: Covering Hillary*. New York: St. Martins, 2001, p. 205.
57. Quoted in Harpaz, *The Girls in the Van: Covering Hillary*. New York: St. Martins, 2001, p. 239.
58. Quoted in Whitney, *Nine and Counting: The Women of the Senate*. New York: Harper Collins, 2001, p. 206–207.
59. Quoted in Clinton, *My Life*. New York: Knopf, 2004, p. 945.
60. Quoted in Whitney, *Nine and Counting: The Women of the Senate*. New York: Harper Collins, 2001, p. 210-211.
61. Quoted in Estrich, *The Case For Hillary Clinton*. New York: Harper Collins, 2005, p. 201.

Chapter 6: Race For The White House

62. Quoted in Anne E. Kornblut, "For The Clinton Candidacy, A Soft Launch," *Washington Post*, January 22, 2007, p. A01.
63. Quoted in Estrich, *The Case For Hillary Clinton*. New York: Harper Collins, 2005, p. 86.

64. Quoted in Karen Tumulty, "Hillary: I Have to Earn Every Vote," *Time*, February 1, 2007, http//www.time.com/0,8816,1584649,00.html

65. Quoted in "The Democrats' Second 2008 Presidential Debate," June 3, 2007, *New York Times*, www.nytimes.com/2007/06/03/us/politics/03demsdebate_transcript.html?

66. Quoted in Anne E. Kornblut, "For The Clinton Candidacy, A Soft Launch," *Washington Post*, January 22, 2007, p. A01.

67. Quoted in Jonathan Alter, "Is America Ready?" *Newsweek*, January 1, 2007, p. 33.

68. Quoted in Estrich, *The Case For Hillary Clinton*. New York: Harper Collins, 2005, p. 140.

1947

Hillary Diane Rodham is born October 26 in Chicago, Illinois.

1950

The Rodham family moves to middle-class Illinois suburb of Park Ridge where Hillary attends public school and church regularly.

1964

Works on Republican Sen. Barry Goldwater's presidential campaign.

1969

Receives Bachelor of Arts degrees from Wellesley College with High Honors as the first student in Wellesley history to give commencement address.

1973

Receives law degree from Yale Law School.

1974

Works for firm doing research to impeach President Richard Nixon.

1975

Marries William Jefferson Clinton on October 11.

1977

Works for Rose Law Firm; Appointed Chair of Legal Services Corporation by President Carter.

1978

Becomes First Lady of the state of Arkansas when husband is sworn in as Governor.

1980

Daughter Chelsea Victoria is born February 27.

1983

Husband reelected Governor and holds office for next ten years; Hillary appointed the head of statewide Education Standards Committee.

1986

Chairs the board of Children's Defense Fund through 1989.

1988

Is named one of the top 100 lawyers in America and again in 1991 by National Law Journal.

1991

Following her husband's announcement to run for president, she campaigns tirelessly on his behalf.

1993

Becomes First Lady of the United States when husband is sworn in as 42nd President on January 20; Is named by President Clinton to Chair the Task Force on National Health Care; Father Hugh Rodham dies; Vince Foster commits suicide.

1994

Task Force culminates in watered down Health Security Act.

1995

Gives speech before UN World Conference on Women in Beijing, China.

1996

Bill Clinton wins reelection; Becomes first wife of a president to testify before a grand jury; *It Takes A Village* is published and becomes a bestseller, audio version wins Grammy.

1998

Bill Clinton is impeached in the House for the Lewinsky scandal; Hillary runs for office.

2000

Elected first woman senator in the state of New York as first former First Lady to hold office.

2001

Sworn-in as senator; Becomes first New York senator to chair Armed Services Committee; September 11 attack.

2003

Autobiography *Living History* is published and becomes a bestseller.

2006

Wins a second term as New York senator by an overwhelming majority.

2007

Announces her candidacy for president on January 20; Launches website of daily blogs outlining position on important topics; Exceeds fundraising expectations of first quarter with $26 million; Debates other declared Democratic candidates.

2008

Presidential primary season begins with several major states moving up their election to the beginning of the year.

For More Information

Books

Madeleine Albright, *Madame Secretary*, New York: Miramax Books, 2003. Autobiography of the first female secretary of state, which also includes several anecdotes that praise the work of Hillary Clinton.

Ann Bausum, *Our Country's Presidents*, Washington DC: National Geographic Society, 2001. Colorful graphics highlight this fact-laden book that covers the history of the American Presidency written for school children. Each president is given a short profile chapter.

P.F. Bentley, *Clinton: Portrait of Victory*. New York: Warner Books, 1993. Time magazine photographer's photo essays on the '92 Clinton presidential campaign is highlighted by many images of Hillary and Bill on the campaign trail as well as occasional personal moments of candor.

Bill Clinton, *My Life*. New York: Knopf, 2004. Autobiography of former President which includes many anecdotes and observations of Hillary Rodham Clinton.

Hillary Rodham Clinton, *Living History*. NY: Simon & Schuster, 2003. Autobiography of the subject told in anecdotal fashion that is both candid and thought provoking.

—— *It Takes A Village: And Other Lessons Children Teach Us*, Simon & Schuster, 1996, NY. Author's lifelong dedication to the cause of children is explained with personal anecdotes and statistics that highlight how the plight of children can be improved.

—— *An Invitation to the White House*, Simon & Schuster, 2000, NY. Oversized book with many impressive photographs accompanying text by Hillary Clinton that details the history of the White House, as well as events, projects and anecdotes involving the eight years the Clintons have spent in the Executive Mansion.

—— *Vital Voices 1997-1999.* Federal Publication, 1999. Collection of speeches made by Hillary Clinton in the three years she was involved in the Vital Voices project dedicated to helping women in the world.

Susan Estrich, *The Case For Hillary Clinton.* New York: Harper Collins, 2005. An in-depth analysis of why Hillary Clinton should run for president. Includes two bibliographies and several statistical charts.

Jim Gullo, *The Importance of Hillary Rodham Clinton.* Farmington Hills: Lucent, 2004. Biography of Hillary Clinton that emphasizes her importance in history with text, photos, timelines and bibliographies.

Patrick S. Halley, *On The Road with Hillary.* New York: Viking, 2002. Author's first person account of working for and with Hillary Clinton as he sets up the details and follows through on events on the campaign trail and in different countries. Includes personal photos.

Beth J. Harpaz, *The Girls in the Van: Covering Hillary.* New York: St. Martins, 2001. Modeled after the book The Boys on the Bus, the author recounts in detail how she covered Hillary Clinton's run for the U.S. Senate in New York.

Kati Marton, *Hidden Power: Presidential Marriages That Shaped Our Recent History.* New York: Random House, 2001. This is an analysis of ten presidential marriages that shaped America's recent history. Includes a full chapter on the Clintons.

S. Michele Nix, ed. *Women at the Podium.* New York: Harper Collins, 2000. A collection of memorable speeches given by prominent women from Ancient Rome to today. The text is divided into sections based on subject and includes Hillary Clinton's speech in honor of the anniversary of the First Women's Rights convention.

Eleanor Roosevelt, *The Autobiography of Eleanor Roosevelt,* New York: Da Capo Press, 1992. A collection of the author's four separate memoirs combined in one volume. An insightful story of the events and accomplishments of the woman Hillary Clinton admires most.

Gail Sheehy, *Hillary's Choice*. New York: Random House, 1999. The first biography of the former first lady while she was still in the White House.

George Stephanopoulos, *All Too Human: A Political Education*. New York: Little, Brown, 1999. This is the author's firsthand account of working on Bill Clinton's presidential campaign and then in his administration with many details and anecdotes concerning Hillary Clinton.

Catherine Whitney, *Nine and Counting: The Women of the Senate*. New York: Harper Collins, 2001. Collection of essays celebrating the women of the U.S. Senate which includes a separate chapter written by Hillary Clinton.

Periodicals

Jonathan Alter, "Hillary's Battle Plan," *Newsweek*, November 27, 2006.

—— "Is America Ready?," *Newsweek*, January 1, 2007.

Carl Sferrazza Anthony, "Hillary Clinton: 'What I Hope To Do As First Lady,'" *Good Housekeeping*, January, 1993.

Molly Ball, "Candidates Pitch Their Cure," *Las Vegas Review-Journal*, March 25, 2007.

Michael Barbaro, "As a Director, Clinton Moved Wal-Mart Board, but Only So Far," *New York Times*, May 20, 2007.

Meredith Berkman, "Hillary Now," *Ladies' Home Journal*, June, 2000.

Margaret Carlson, "All Eyes On Hillary," *Time*, September 14, 1992.

James Carville and Mark J. Penn, "The Power of Hillary," *Washington Post*, July 2, 2006.

Howard G. Chua-Eoan, Nina Burleigh, Linda Kramer, "Power Mom," *People*, January 25, 1993.

Eleanor Clift, "I Think We're Ready," *Newsweek*, February 3, 1992.

Jonathan Darman, "His New Role," *Newsweek*, May 28, 2007.

Michael Finnegan, "Giuliani and Clinton stay in the lead," *LA Times*, June 12, 2007.

Dan Gilgoff, "Hillary's Dilemma," *US News & World Report*, November 20, 2006.

Jed Graham, "Sen. Clinton At Odds With Base Over Her '02 Vote For Iraq War," *Investor's Business Daily*, February 16, 2007.

Patrick Healy, "Mindful of Past, Clinton Cultivates the Military," *New York Times*, March 27, 2007.

—— "Clinton Camp Turns to a Star in Money Race," *New York Times*, March 31, 2007.

Jack Hitt, "Harpy, Hero, Heretic, Hillary," *Mother Jones,* January/February 2007.

Landon Y. Jones, "Road Warriors," *People,* July 2, 1992.

Jill Lawrence, "Why Some Democrats Worry that Clinton Can't Win," *USA Today*, January 22, 2007.

—— Question for Hillary: What Will Bill's Impact Be?," *USA Today,* March 29, 2007.

Rod McCullom, "Behind the Gay-Friendly Faces," *The Advocate,* April 10, 2007.

Susannah Meadows, "What Are Hillary's Religious Beliefs?," *Newsweek*, February 12, 2007.

Dan Morain and Scott Braun, "Clinton Rakes in Early Money," *LA Times,* April 2, 2007.

John O'Neil, "Hillary Rodham Clinton: Seeking a Return to the White House," *New York Times*, March 12, 2007.

Susan Schindehette, "Hillary, Act II," *People*, July 1, 2002.

Gail Sheehy, "What Hillary Wants," *Vanity Fair,* May 5, 1992.

Chris Smith, "The Lady in the Bubble," New York, November 13, 2006.

James B. Stewart, "On the Road to Scandal," *Time*, March 18, 1996.

Karen Tumulty, "Turning Fifty," *Time*, October 20, 1997.

—— "The Better Half," *Time*, December 28, 1998.

—— "Ready To Run," *Time*, August 28, 2006.

—— "Hillary: I Have to Earn Every Vote," *Time*, February 1, 2007.

Jill Zuckman, "I Am Woman," *Chicago Tribune,* March 6, 2007.

Web Sites

Hillary Clinton.com (http://www.hillaryclinton.com). The official website of Hillary Clinton's presidential campaign with blogs, updates, links and videos of the campaign. Highlights are the daily "Hillcasts" of the candidate on the campaign trail.

Hillary Rodham Clinton, Senator From New York (http://clinton.senate.gov). Hillary Clinton's official website as U.S. Senator, it features career highlights, video downloads and blogs of her tenure as senator. Also includes a forum in which constituents can contact the Senator.

Hillary Hub (http://www.hillaryhub.com/). A Website dedicated to Hillary's presidential election campaign with daily links to events on the campaign trail and media stories.

Hillary is 44 (http://www.HillaryIs44.org). This site is dedicated to making Hillary the 44th President of the United Sates. Includes daily blogs from supporters and updates on media events.

Adams, Ruth, 24
advice to young women, 11
Afghanistan
  supporting military action in,
    75, 83
  visits to, 83
Al Qaeda, 83
Albright, Madeleine, 58, 60
American Bar Association, 47
Angel One (medical helicopter
  service), 44
Arafat, Suha, 70
Arkansas
  education reforms, 44–47
  health care, 41–42
  Hillary in, 35–47
  See also First Lady (Arkansas)
Arkansas Advocates for Children
  and Families, 37
Arkansas Education Standards
  Committee, 44–45
Arkansas Woman of the Year,
  45
Armed Services Committee,
  chair of, *73*, 74, 75
astronaut, dream of being an,
  17–18

Bell, Terrence, 46
*Beyond the Best Interests of the
  Child* (Freud, et al.), 32
Biden, Joe, 84
Bin Laden, Osama, 75, 83
Bond, Christopher, *62*
Braun, Carol Moseley, 79
breaking down barriers, 8, *9*

bully, dealing with a, 17
Bush, George H. W., 48, 76,
  81
Bush administration
  conflict with, 76, 84–86
  health care problems under,
    84

Caraway, Hattie Wyatt, 79
Carnegie Council on Children,
  32
Carter, Jimmy, working on
  presidential campaign of, 37
The Case Against Hillary Clinton
  (Noonan), 88
The Case for Hillary Clinton
  (Estrich), 88
CDF. *See* Children's Defense
  Fund, The
children's advocate, *10*, 10–11,
  19, 58, 65
  founder of the Arkansas
    Advocates for Children and
    Families, 37
  as a law student, 27–28
  as a young person, 18
Children's Defense Fund, The
  (CDF), 28, 32, 47
Chisholm, Shirley, 79
Clinton, Bill, 29, *31*, *34*, 35
  attraction to, 30, *34*
  campaign, Congressional, 35
  campaign for presidency, 48,
    49
  campaign for state attorney
    general, 35

campaign for state governor, first, 39

campaign for state governor, second, 44

as governor of Arkansas, 40

impeachment, 63–64

marriage to Hillary, 37, 63, 65

meeting Hillary's family, 30–31

presidential election night party, 47

relationship with Monica Lewinsky, 63, 64

Clinton, Chelsea Victoria
birth, 38, 42, 42
privacy, 41, 43

Clinton, Hillary Rodham
in Arkansas, 35–47
campaign for Senate, 66–73
campaign for the White House, 77–88
college years, 22–32, 23
as First Lady (Arkansas), 39–49
as First Lady (U.S.), 50–65
important date in the life of, 94–96
as Senator of New York, 73–76
youth, 12–22

Clinton, Hillary, photographs of, 9, 10, 19, 45, 51, 68, 85
with Bill, 20, 31, 34, 36, 42, 47

Clinton, Roger, 30

Clinton, Virginia, 29–30, 31–32

community project through Church youth group, 20–21

Conservatism, defined, 14

corporate boards, sitting in, 46

debates with Rick Lazio, 71, 71–72

Democratic, defined, 14

Democratic Party
Clinton, Bill, and, 48
replacement of Moynihan and, 66–67

Dodd, Chris, 84

Doyle, Patti Solis, 82, 82, 87

Edelman, Marian Wright, 27, 27, 32
Children's Defense Fund and, 28

education
developing early childhood education, 45
reforms in Arkansas, 44–47

Edwards, John, 84

Estrich, Susan, 88

Europe, vacation in, 41

Ferraro, Geraldine, 79

Filegate, 57

finances investigation, 62

First Lady (Arkansas), 39–39
balancing legal work and duties of, 8, 40

First Lady (U.S.), 50–65
duties as, 72
speaking engagements, 58

Foster, Vince, 54

Freud, Anna, 32

Frist, Bill, 75
fundraising
  for the 2008 campaign, 77,
    82, 86–88, 87
  as a youth, 15

gender, presidential race and,
  86
Gingrich, Newt, 61
  working with, 75
Giuliani, Rudy
  mayor of New York City,
    75
  New York Republican
    Senatorial candidate, 67,
    69, 70
  presidential candidate, 78
Goldwater, Barry, 21
goodwill ambassador, 58
Gore, Al, 81
Grammy Award for Best Spoken
  Word Recording, 61

Hammerschmidt, John Paul,
  35
Harvard Law School, 26
health care
  in Arkansas, 41–42
  as issue in 2008 presidential
    race, 84–86
  problems under Bush admin-
    istration, 84
health care reform, 52–56
  failure of, 11
  Health Care Task Force, 11, 52
  legislation, 56, 57–58
  speaking tour and, 55–56
  testifying before Congress, 54,
    56
  work as Senator on, 75

Health Security Act (1994),
  57–58
Hidden Power (Marton), 50
higher education. See Wellesley;
  Yale Law School
Hillaryclinton.com, 78
HIPPY. See Home Instruction
  Program for Preschool
  Youngsters
historical preservation, 65
Home Instruction Program for
  Preschool Youngsters (HIPPY),
  45

Ickes, Harold, 67
impeachment of Bill Clinton,
  63–64
Indiana, working on Carter's
  campaign in, 37
Internet, campaigning and, 77
  Hillaryclinton.com, 78, 78, 80
Iraq war, 83–84
  visits to Iraq, 83
  vote for invasion of Iraq, 83
It Takes A Village (Clinton), 10,
  59, 61

Johnson, Lyndon, 21
Johnson, Samuel, 56
Jones, Don, 20–21, 22, 46

Kennedy, John F., 21
Kerry, John, 81
Kiley, Kevin, 73
King, Martin Luther, Jr.
  assassination, 24
  meeting, 21
Koop, C. Everett, 56

lawyer, career as

at the Children's Defense Fund, 32

at Rose Law Firm, 8, 37, *38*

during Watergate, 32–33

Lazio, Rick, 71, 71–72

leadership ability, natural, 15–16, 18

Left Wing/Right Wing, defined, 14

Legal Services Corporation, 37

Lewinsky, Monica, 63

Liberalism, defined, 14

The Listening Tour, 70

Living History (Clinton), *80*
  on attraction to Bill, 30
  on childhood, 17
  as test of reaction to presidential run, 80–81

Marton, Kati, 50

McDougal, Jim, 61

McGovern, George, working on the campaign of, 30, *31*

McRae, Tom, 47–48

Methodist Church, influence of, 18, 20–21

Mohony, Roger Cardinal, *19*

Mondale, Walter, 28

Moynihan, Daniel Patrick, 66, 67, 68

name
  changing to married name, 44
  using maiden name, 42–43

National Law Journal, 47

New York City, campaigning in, 69

New York State, campaigning in, 69, 69–70

1950s, the United States in the, 16–17

Nixon, Richard, 32

Noonan, Peggy, 83, 88

Obama, Barack, 78, *81*

Office of Independent Counsel (OIC), 61–62

opportunistic, accusations of being, 10

organizational skills, 35, 40

parents, 12–16
  politics and, 21
  values of, 15–16

partisan/bipartisan, defined, 14

Pelosi, Nancy, 79

Perot, Ross, 48

political opponents, working with, 11

political policy *versus* public advocacy, 34–35, 38

Poor People's Campaign, CDF and, 28

presidential campaign (Bill) of 1992, 48
  Hillary and, 49

presidential campaign of 2008, 77–88, *85*
  debate with Obama, *81*
  Doyle as campaign manager, 82, *82*, 87

presidential race of 2004, 81

presidential race of 2008
  issues in, 84–86
  uniqueness of, 77–78

press, conflict with, 11, 51, 53

public advocacy *versus* political policy, 34–35, 38

public service, pitfalls of choosing, 74

Rankin, Jeannette, 79
Republican
  in college, 22
  defined, 14
  in high school, 21
Rich, Marc, pardon of, 66
Richardson, Bill, 78
Rodham, Dorothy Emma
  Howell, 12–13, *13*, *16*, 17,
  24
Rodham, Hugh, 13–15, *16*,
  24–25, 53–54
  Clinton, Bill, and, 31
Rodham, Hugh (brother), 15
Rodham, Tony, 15, 18
Romney, Mitt, 78
Roosevelt, Eleanor, 58, 60
Roosevelt, Franklin Delano, 60,
  61
Rose Law Firm (Little Rock), 37,
  38, *38*, 39, 44, 54
Rural Health Advisory
  Committee (Arkansas), 41–42

Saddam Hussein, 83
scandals, 57–58
  Whitewater, 61–63
Schumer, Chuck, 69, 74
Senate Whitewater Committee
  hearings, *62*
Senator of New York State,
  73–76, 83
  announcing candidacy,
    67–68
  campaign, 69–72
  election, 72–73
  second term, 75–76
September 11, 2001, 74–75
Smith, Margaret Chase, 79
spirituality, *20*, 20–21, 67
Stanton, Elizabeth Cady, 79

Starr, Ken, 62, 63
Stephanopoulos, George, 48,
  49, 62
style change, political
  campaigns and, 39–40, 44

terminology, political, 14
terrorist attacks of September
  11, 2001, 74–75
Today (television show), 63–64
Travelgate, 57
Tribou, George, 67
Tripp, Linda, 63
Troopergate, 57

United Nations World
  Conference on Women
  (Beijing)
  discussions about, 61
  speech at, 58, 60
University of Arkansas School of
  Law, teaching at, 33, 35

Vietnam War, opposition to, 24

Wallace, Mike, 60
war on terrorism, 83
Washington Research Project,
  CDF and, 28
Watergate break-in, 32–33
  on staff of the Senate Judiciary
    committee, 33
Wellesley College, 22, 23
  commencement address, 8,
    24–25
Wesley, John, 18
White House
  Hillary in the East Room, *51*
  Hillary's office in the West
    Wing, 53
  renovations, 65

website, 65
White House Conference on Childcare (1997), 65
Whitewater scandal, 61–63
Wilson, Marie, 86
women in the workplace, enhancing the role of, 46–47
women politicians, pioneering, 79

women's rights advocate, 58
Woodhull, Victoria, 79
Woodward, Bob, 54

Yale Child Study Center, 32
Yale Law School, 26–32
Yale Review of Law and Social Action, 27
Young Republican, 22

Dwayne Epstein was born in Brooklyn, New York and grew up in southern California. His first professional writing credit was in 1982, writing newspaper film reviews and year-end analysis of popular culture.

Nationally, he has been a regular contributor to several film magazines since 1996. Internationally, he contributed to Bill Krohn's film book *Serious Pleasures* in 1997, which saw publication in Europe. Mr. Epstein has had several children's books published since 2000 and is currently writing a biography on actor Lee Marvin. Mr. Epstein also authored *People In the News: Adam Sandler, People In the News: Will Ferrell, People In the News: Hilary Swank* and *History Makers: Lawmen of the Old West,* all for Lucent Books. He lives in Long Beach with his girlfriend Barbara and too many books on movie history.